Krishna

The Living God of Braj

Krishna

The Living God of Braj

D. Anand

ABHINAV PUBLICATIONS
abhinav publications

First published in India 1992

Publishers

Shakti Malik
Abhinav Publications
E-37, Hauz Khas
New Delhi-110016

ISBN 81-7017-280-2

Designers PARSHURAM PRASAD
ANIL TATO
Consultant RAM DHAMIJA

Printers

Mehta Offset Works
Naraina Industrial Area
New Delhi

Contents

To

PRAKASH

my wife

&

AKSHAY

my grandson

FOREWORD

Krishna, the living God of Braj, inspires and evokes love and joy as much as He demands faith, devotion and, above all, surrender. Krishna is that mythic image of the Indian consciousness which is ever-present, moving in and out, playing hide-and-seek with time past and time future. To try and seek either historicity or to weave a pattern of rationality is to confine the power of the moving clouds in the sky to measurable volumes of geometry. Studies on Krishna are, therefore, as innumerable as the visions which this mythic image invokes in the minds of those who are drawn to it.

Whether historically true or not, Krishna was born in the Braj Kshetra and He moved to Dwarka later. What is important is that the whole Kshetra of Braj is sacred because of the mythic Krishna permeates the Kshetra. Here and now, the lanes and bylanes of Vrindavan reverberate in the inner ears of the devotees with the flute of Krishna. Groves and shrubs are made sacred each day anew through faith and devotion of the Bhakatas. The loves of Krishna and the gopis and Krishna and Radha are recreated each day, each moment.

In whatever hoary antiquity the myth was created or the historical figure born, Krishna of Harivansh Purana and the Vishnu Purana is rejuvenated in the Shrimad Bhagvat. This already takes nearly a thousand years. Another 500 years passed before the Kshetra of Braj comes alive with new vigour and renewal of the imagery of Krishna. Now it is the centre of the Krishna lore and Indians from all parts of India converged, as they converge today, to be in communion with this living presence.

Dr. Anand has been magnetically pulled and attracted by this living God, as many others. The book is a sheer labour of love in which he explores the physical, historical, ritual and artistic dimensions of the Braj Kshetra. The joy of playfulness of Krishna, the fairs and the festivities, the medieval temples and the paintings, the contemporary music and dance, the floor drawings of the Sanjhis, are captured through a lense with a loving eye. I have no doubt that anyone who reads this book and sees the photographs will respond to the enchanted world of Krishna, the Living God.

September 12, 1992 — Dr. Kapila Vatsyayan
New Delhi

Introduction

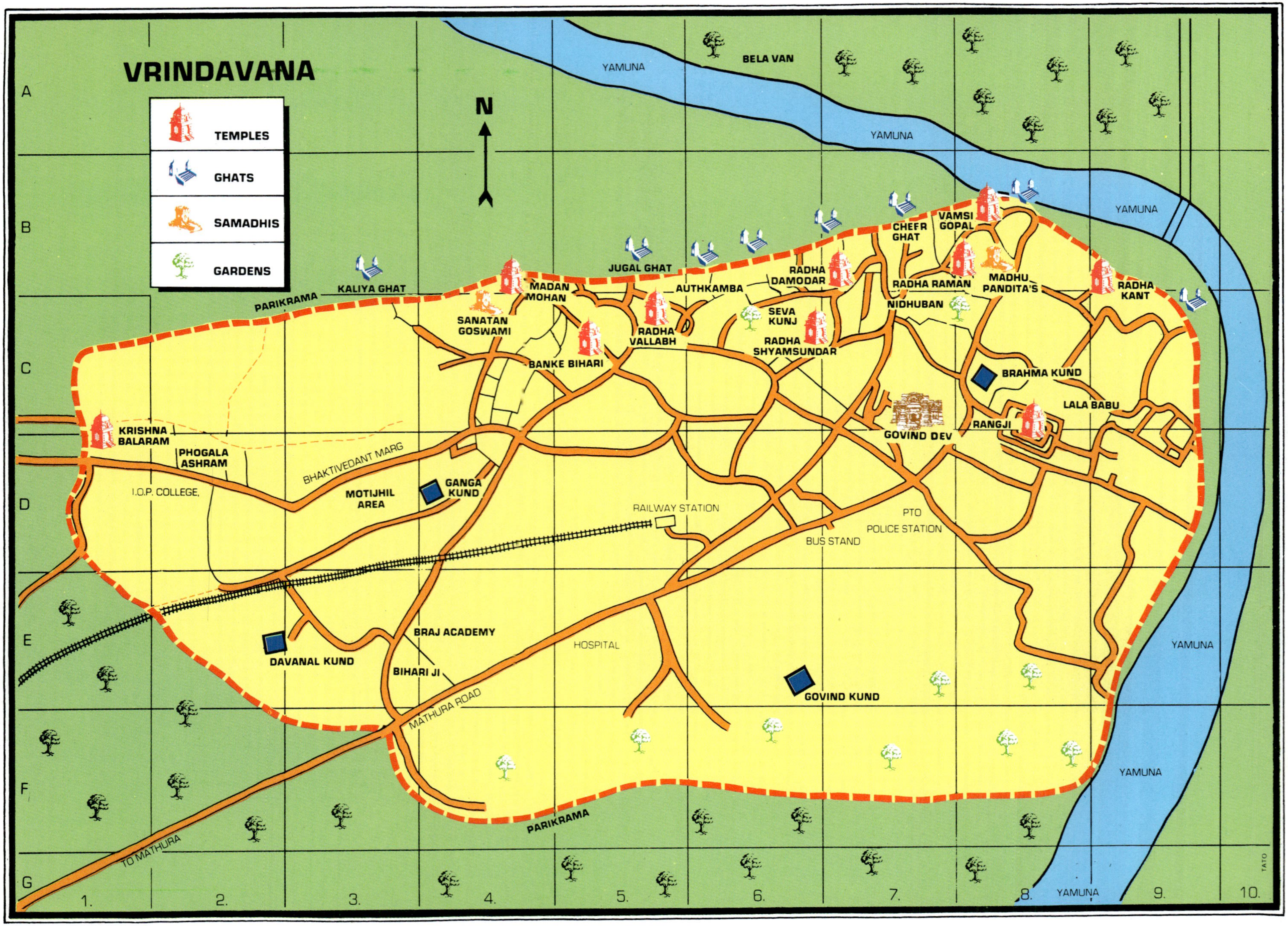
VRINDAVANA
TEMPLES
GHATS
SAMADHIS
GARDENS
N
YAMUNA
BELA VAN
YAMUNA
YAMUNA
KALIYA GHAT
PARIKRAMA
JUGAL GHAT
AUTHKAMBA
RADHA DAMODAR
CHEFR GHAT
VAMSI GOPAL
RADHA RAMAN
MADHU PANDITA'S
RADHA KANT
MADAN MOHAN
SANATAN GOSWAMI
RADHA VALLABH
SEVA KUNJ
RADHA SHYAMSUNDAR
NIDHUBAN
BANKE BIHARI
BRAHMA KUND
LALA BABU
RANGJI
GOVIND DEV
KRISHNA BALARAM
PHOGALA ASHRAM
BHAKTIVEDANT MARG
I.O.P. COLLEGE,
MOTIJHIL AREA
GANGA KUND
RAILWAY STATION
PTO
POLICE STATION
BUS STAND
BRAJ ACADEMY
DAVANAL KUND
BIHARI JI
HOSPITAL
GOVIND KUND
MATHURA ROAD
YAMUNA
YAMUNA
PARIKRAMA
TO MATHURA
YAMUNA
TATO
A
B
C
D
E
F
G
1.
2.
3.
4.
5.
6.
7.
8.
9.
10.

This work on Krishna of Braj is the fulfilment of a dream nursed for almost forty years. My initial curiosity in Krishna was aroused in nineteen hundred and forty-six. I had observed the rural folk of Gursarai in district Jhansi wearing country-made shoes with the motif of a peacock feather embroidered on them. It was unmistakably meant to depict the headwear of Krishna! The people of the village considered themselves to be the descendants of the legendary King Chediraj Shishupal, who had been killed by Krishna when the Rajsuya Yagya was being held by Yudhisthara. The people being the subjects of Shishupal held the enemy of their king in perpetual disgrace. This interpretation produced a powerful impact on my mind. It only added to my curiosity to know more about Krishna who is loved, venerated, respected, and even disrespected, in the same country, India.

The other reason for undertaking this venture came from a perusal of illustrated books on Krishna that have been published in India and abroad. Many of these books use the Krishna theme to present paintings of different styles, such as Kangra or Mewar. The others describe a variety of performing arts using the Krishna theme. All these books have limitations. They are unable to bring to the millions of people in India and abroad the story of Krishna, the Living God whose vibrant thoughts bring to many a sense of peace and joy. This is very apparent in Braj, the land of Krishna's birth, where chanting the name of Shri Krishna and Shri Radha forms an essential part of the everyday existence of the local people. They glean a sense of happiness and satisfaction by simply living in Braj. I felt that a camera is the most suitable medium to convey this living aspect of people's interaction of Radha and Krishna in day-to-day life.

The present effort provides visual images of various temples and places associated with the Krishna legend. Only a camera can effectively capture the beauty of the temples of Govindji or Madan Mohan in Vrindavan, or the panoramic oriental landscape of Radhakund.

Many of these places are at present in a state of neglect and decay and may disappear altogether. This book attempts to provide a graphic and pictorial record of the places identified in the Puranas or other ancient literature for their association with the legend of Shri Krishna.

For purposes of description, the book has been divided into five sections:

Places: The photographs cover the important sites associated with the Krishna legend in Braj. The accompanying maps of Braj (area: 268 sq km) and Vrindavan will help in identifying the important sites that have been covered.

Temples: Mathura, Vrindavan and almost all the villages in their neighbourhood are full of temples for worshipping Shri Radha and Shri Krishna. The main temples of Mathura, Vrindavan and other important places have been photographed. This would give some idea of the varied forms in which Krishna is worshipped in a cross-section of the temples of Braj.

It has not been possible to photograph the presiding deity of all the famous temples. In some, like Bihariji's at Vrindavan, taking of photographs is strictly prohibited. At other places, it is a matter of discretion of the priest who performs puja. In all such cases, the sensitivities of the local priests have been respected.

Famous Devotees: Braj has historically attracted people from all over India to come in search of divine vision and contemplation. This tradition has continued to the present period, during which Shri Bhaktivedanta Swami Prabhupada came to Braj to seek enlightenment and spread the message of love and devotion throughout the world. This section provides an account of these devotees, the places they stayed in and their contribution to Krishnaism and the cultural heritage of Braj.

Fairs and Festivals: Krishna and his divine consort are the central theme in all the festivals held in Braj. Some are exclusively related to their presence, such as the birthdays of Radha and Krishna. The others like 'Holi' develop a unique flavour because of the association with Shri Radha. The festivals therefore result in both devotion and gay abandon which are captured by the camera in this section.

Creative and Performing Arts: According to tradition, Krishna was also known to be a great dancer. His flute charmed the gops and gopis and has been immortalised in the romantic poems and songs of famous poets. The local artists cover a wide range of art forms such as making a house of flowers or designing motifs on earth with dry, coloured powder. This section covers the range of artistic activities that are mostly associated with Krishna and are peculiar to the land of Braj.

The work on this book started about five years ago. It has taken almost four years since the work began with shooting the first sequence of pictures in Vrindavan. Since then my camera and I have traversed the length and breadth of Braj. There were moments of despair, sometimes frustration, but there was always an overriding feeling of confidence that one day the work would be completed. That day has come and it would be the end of the trail that started five years ago, and was dreamt about 40 years ago. I will now miss visiting the familiar faces all over Braj of those who have been kind and have shared their thoughts, wisdom and hospitality to make this voyage come through. All those faces come alive as I pen these words. I can only thank all my friends and Brajbasis who gave me the strength and the opportunity to complete this work.

After the initial exploratory work, it was realised that it could not be undertaken single-handed. It would be difficult to photograph places and people unless one knew the background of the places to be photographed, and also, unless one had the concurrence of the local people/pundits. It therefore became essential to have a team of persons familiar with Braj and the writings related to this land. I was lucky to have met a large number of people from all walks of life, who shared their views with me and provided help, often going out of their way. It is not easy to remember and thank every one of them. However, it would be remiss of me not to specially mention Pundit Ramesh Chand Goswami of Barsana, Shri Pulin Goswami, Shri Shri Vats, Shri Vrindavan Bihari, U.B. group for their support and Smt. Reba Som whose valued comments and help facilitated this work.

The most indispensable help came from a charming young couple, Dr. Sadhana and Dr. Kumud Kulshrestha. Sadhana, a keen photographer, with doctoral research on various aspects of Vrindavan, took personal interest in this work. Her major contribution has been the research conducted on the Krishna legend which has been vital for my photography. She has done this very creditably with some assistance from her husband, Dr. Kulshrestha.

During the course of this project, I often felt lost because of the magnitude of the work to be undertaken. It required visiting remote and little-known places. It was also important to identify the most opportune time to photograph an event or a place, such as temples at a particular time or a special occasion. The travel back and forth from Delhi to Mathura and Vrindavan meant expenses, not easily anticipated. Hence, an attempt was made to apply for a grant to cover the production cost. This exercise has provided a new insight into the existing interest in art and the cultural heritage of India.

There are practically no funds for a rank outsider to venture on such a project. After a repeated 'no' from many institutions and organisations in India and elsewhere, I decided to do it on my own. The Krishna project became a full-time occupation. The moral support for completing this work came from many familiar as also many unknown faces. My daughter Mridu and her husband Satish, as also my son Pradeep and his wife Rohini, encouraged me to complete the work. They all, in their own way, have helped in the preparation of the manuscript. Recharging of flagging spirits was provided by meeting Indian friends, many of them abroad, specially in the USA. The keen interest shown at the various illustrated talks on Braj that were organised in the USA was most encouraging.

New Delhi
August 1990

D. ANAND

1. Sunset, Govardhan. (On end paper)

2. Krishna, son of Nand Baba, chief of herdsmen. A popular image in Braj. (On page 1)

3. Shri Krishna: lifesize deity in Sadhu Bela Temple, Vrindavan. (On page 6)

4. Shrimad Bhagvat: the holy book and fountain-head of the Krishna legend. (On page 9)

Braj

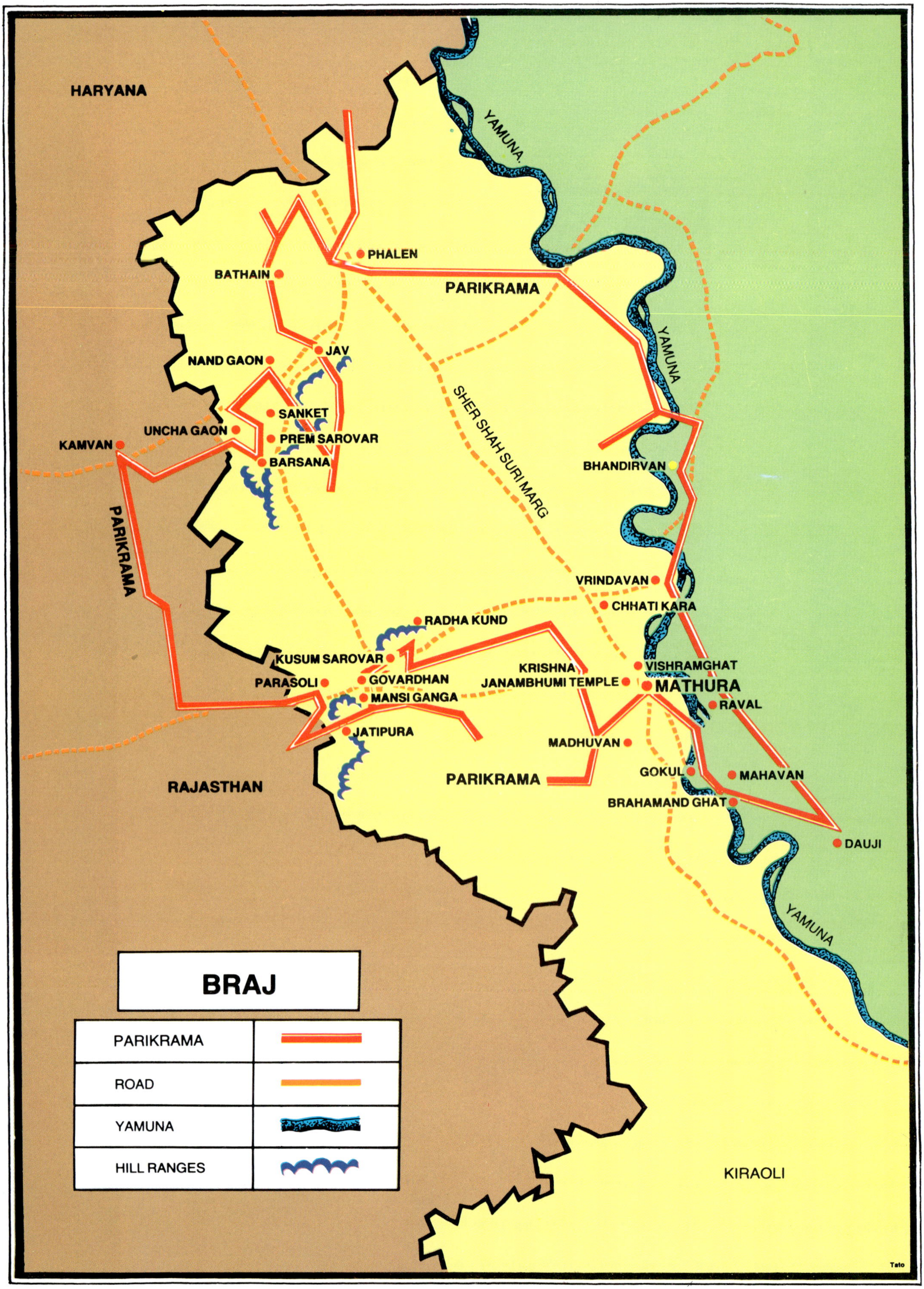

HARYANA
YAMUNA.
PHALEN
BATHAIN
PARIKRAMA
JAV
NAND GAON
YAMUNA
SHER SHAH SURI MARG
SANKET
UNCHA GAON
PREM SAROVAR
KAMVAN
BARSANA
BHANDIRVAN
PARIKRAMA
VRINDAVAN
CHHATI KARA
RADHA KUND
KUSUM SAROVAR
KRISHNA
JANAMBHUMI TEMPLE
VISHRAMGHAT
MATHURA
PARASOLI
GOVARDHAN
MANSI GANGA
RAVAL
JATIPURA
MADHUVAN
GOKUL
MAHAVAN
PARIKRAMA
RAJASTHAN
BRAHAMAND GHAT
DAUJI
YAMUNA
BRAJ
PARIKRAMA
ROAD
YAMUNA
HILL RANGES
KIRAOLI
Tato

The name Braj conjures up a thousand images of the mythological, cultural and spiritual heritage of the Braj land. Covering 84 *kos* (268 km) in northern India, Braj land has Mathura as its nucleus. According to Puranic descriptions, Braj extended to Bhuvanvan in the north, Jahvan in the south, Hasyavan in the east and Apharvan in the west.[1] The Skand Purana describes Braj as a station for herdsmen.[2] It has steadily attracted people from all walks of life, people who have renounced their worldly life and settled down to a life of austere simplicity in Braj in the vicinity of Vrindavan. What is the compelling attraction of this land? The answer lies in the environment, the mythological and historical past of the region and its people.

From the mythological period to the present, the land of Braj has been called by various names. Mentioned in chronological order these are Madhyadesh, Brahmanishi, Shursen, Mathuramandal and Braj.

Two mythological references help to define the location of the land, as also to offer an explanation for the name 'Braj'. According to the Puranic description, Lord Krishna once went to visit Shri Radha, who, however, was absent. Instead Virija, a playmate of Shri Radha, welcomed the Lord. Krishna made advances and Virija responded. When, after some time, they heard the footsteps of Shri Radha, the Lord disappeared. Shri Radha noticed the love-lorn mood of Virija and immediately cursed her to become a river. Virija is the river Yamuna and the area she flows through is now called Braj.[3]

Another episode concerns Lord Brahma. He had apparently stolen one hundred thousand calves, cows and gops of Nand Baba (Krishna's foster father). Krishna, according to the story, immediately created afresh an even number of cows, calves and gops to allay the fears of other gops and also to demonstrate to Brahma his own divine power. The calves roamed in the area defined as Braj Kshetra for about a year.[4] Brahma was mystified at seeing the miracle and returned the original cows, calves and gops to the rightful owner.

5. Krishna and the Gopes — Kangra Bhagvat Purana, early 19th century. Courtesy: National Museum, New Delhi. (On page 17)

The mythological importance of Braj stems from the fact that it was in this area that Krishna was born and where he gradually displayed his divine powers in destroying *asuras* (demons), thereby restoring peace and social order. The sanctity of Braj is also associated with its legendary descent from Golok.[5] It is stated that when Vishnu, residing in Golok, planned to descend on earth as 'Krishna', he ordered a part of Golok (268 sq km), Yamuna and Govardhan to descend on earth as well. This part is the area described as Braj.[6] According to believers, this is a most sacred land and is not governed by the natural laws of destruction and creation. The scriptures have recorded that the land was so sacred that the gods would descend to walk on it and to cover themselves with its celestial dust, Braj *Raj.* Both Vishnu Purana and Bhagvat Purana eulogise the spiritual aspect of Mathuramandal with Brajmandal. The land of Mathura was considered so sacred that it was said that if someone overheard the name 'Mathura', he was absolved of all his sins.

Vishnu Rahasya describes the natural settings and environment of Braj. The woods (Van) of Braj are described as parts of the divine form and hence deemed very sacred.

According to this description, while Mathura was the Hriday (heart), Madhuvan the Nabhi (navel), Kumudtalvan the Stan Yugal (breasts), Mandir Kokilavan the Hast Yugal (both hands), Khandirbhadravan the Kandhe (both shoulders), Vrindavan the Mastishk (forehead) and Kamvan was the Thuddi (chin).

In the Brahmanic scriptures (Puranas), detailed account of the land of Braj can also be found.

Thus in the Harivansh Purana, Braj is described as the land where Nand and his clan lived, where Krishna had spent his childhood.[7]

In the Skand Purana, Maharishi Sandilya described Braj as a land with transcendental and spiritual qualities.[8] This is the land where the divine *leela* of Krishna was performed with its two facets, the actual or real leela, which, to the people in the Braj area, was an everyday occurrence, and the customary leela which was seen in Golok.

Shrimad Bhagvat, the most important treatise on Krishna, has described Braj as having two parts: Brahadvan, which was the abode of Nand Baba, where some of the early leelas of Krishna took place, such as the elimination of demons named Putna, Shakat and Tarnavrat, or where Krishna, the butter thief, was tied with a rope to prevent him from stealing butter, and Vrindavan, with Govardhan in the vicinity.[9] According to Padam Purana, Vrindavan was the permanent home of Lord Vishnu.[10] The vibrant, devotional atmosphere of Vrindavan is conducive to a mood of worship and meditation.

The sanctity attached to Vrindavan is illustrated from an amusing episode recorded in the Puranas. As the story goes, sage Narada, in the course of his travels on earth, visited Prayagraj (Allahabad), situated at the confluence of the three holy rivers (Ganga, Yamuna and Saraswati). Prayagraj was therefore considered the most important among all places of pilgrimage in India. The sage Narada provoked Prayagraj by asking why it was that Vrindavan had not recognised its primacy and offered it homage. Narada suggested that Prayagraj raise this question with Lord Vishnu himself.

Prayagraj visited Lord Vishnu and sought confirmation about the supremacy of his status as the most important of all religious places. Vishnu explained that there was no challenge to the status of Prayagraj from Vrindavan, because Vrindavan was not merely a religious place but the home of the Lord himself.

The added importance of the land of Braj is due to the alleged descent there of Vishnu, as Krishna.[11] Most of the childhood leela of Krishna was said to have been performed in Braj. Lord Vishnu is visualised and venerated as the 'child Krishna'. It is this incarnation of Krishna which was the most human, adorable and loved. In the religious scriptures and the devotional songs and poems, Braj has come to assume a special spiritual importance.

It is believed that there are three crore minute Vishnus in the dust of Vrindavan. Some of the devotional sects following Krishnaism go to the extent of applying the dust of Braj to their foreheads. The love which the people residing in Braj have for this land is vividly portrayed by the poet Raskhan.[12] He says:

— should I be a man, then let me, Raskhan, mingle with the herds of cattle,

— if a beast, then how should I live but ever grazing amongst the cows of Nand,

— if a stone, then a part of the Govardhan hill like an umbrella for protection of the Braj against the wrath of Lord Indra,

— if a bird, then let me dwell for ever in the boughs of the Kadamb tree on the banks of the Yamuna.

Braj suffered decay after the departure of Krishna for Dwarka. Even during Krishna's time the place was subjected to repeated attacks by the troops of Jarasandh, who wanted to avenge the killing of his son-in-law Kans by Krishna. According to tradition, Bajranabh, the great grandson of Krishna, had discussed the problem of growing decay with Parikshit, son of Abhimanyu and grandson of Arjun. Parikshit approached Sandilya Rishi to obtain more information on Braj. The Rishi revealed the mythological legacy of Braj and asked Bajranabh to establish settlements at six places, namely, Govardhan, Deegh, Mathura, Mahavan, Nandgaon and Barsana.[13]

Archeological and historical evidence indicates that Braj in general and Mathura in particular were of great importance during the time of the Kushanas, the Nagas and the Mauryas. Mathura and the places around it in Braj came to be ransacked by invaders such as the Huns, the Sakas (Scythians), the Greeks, and again later, by Mahmud Ghaznavi, Sikander Lodi, Allauddin Khilji and many others. The persistence of these attacks however had little effect on the devotional aura of the land.

A journey through present-day Braj however shows disappointing changes in the physical environment. Braj, traditionally reputed to have 12 vans (forests), 24 *upvans* (small forests), and many *tals* (ponds), today has a receding Yamuna skirting it, shrinking forests and polluted ponds.

Krishna

EXIT
CANARA BANK
CANARA BANK

According to legend, it was in the royal dungeons of King Kans in Braj that Krishna was born to Vasudev and Devaki for the purpose of delivering the people from oppression to a just social order.[14] Who was this godhead Krishna? A rich and colourful web of imagery has been woven around the figure by religious scriptures such as the Puranas and Shrimad Bhagvat, as also the writings of scholars and saints, such as Shri Chaitanya, Sanatan Goswami, Swami Prabhupada and others. They have helped create a multi-faceted image of Krishna as he constantly flits from the realm of history to mythology. As one travels through Mathura today one cannot but be touched by the pulsating reality and relevance of the Krishna legend in the day-to-day existence of the local people. The attempt here is to project, in broad outline, certain aspects of this legend to provide the necessary backdrop to the pictorial presentation of the land of Krishna.

According to Shrimad Bhagvat, Vishnu Purana and other Puranas, Krishna was born after midnight on the eighth day of the sixth month of Hindu Calendar, in a jail of Kans, the tyrant ruler of Mathura. The scriptures also mention that Krishna appeared before Vasudev and Devaki in the jail cell in his divine form as the four-headed Vishnu. Seeing this, Devaki worshipped him, and at the same time implored him to conceal his divine form. Conceding Devaki's wishes, Krishna appeared as a newly born infant. This Puranic description is a part of the leela of Krishna as an *Avatar*.

Who is an Avatar? An Avatar is a divine incarnation on earth, born with the purpose of uplifting mankind from misery. Shri Aurobindo, a philosopher sage of the twentieth century, giving reasons for the Avatar's descent, states: "The reason for which Avatars descend is to raise up man again and again, developing in him a higher and ever higher humanity, a greater and yet greater development of the divine being until our toil is done, our work is accomplished . . . even in this material universe."[15]

6. Keshav Dev, the deity of Keshav Dev Temple. The original deity is stated to have been installed by Bajranabh, the great-grandson of Krishna. (On page 25)

7. Bhagvat Bhawan, located at the place believed to be the birth-place of Krishna at Mathura.

8. Bird's-eye view of Shri Krishna Janmabhumi Complex, Mathura.

9. Nratya Gopal, Vrindavan.

9

10. Marble pavilion in the underground prison cell where Vasudeva and Devaki were kept. Krishna is said to have been born in this prison cell.

Krishna in his own words to Arjun, in the Bhagvat Gita, explains that the purpose of his descent on earth was "to restore the religious and social order and destroy the forces of evil that create chaos and destruction."[16] The scriptures and the epics like the Mahabharat provide ample examples of how the forces of evil were pitted against the forces of good championed by Krishna in an Armageddon-like fight to the finish.

Krishna of Mahabharat fame has provided a very powerful image to the people in India. He revealed the Gita, which is an immensely appealing Hindu scripture. Krishna serves only as a charioteer to Arjun during the eighteen days of the epic battle. Yet his influence in shaping the battle and its strategy is seen throughout the eighteen days and thereafter. This powerful image of Krishna of Mahabharat has led some to visualise that he is different from the Krishna of Braj. This view is however not supported by even references in the epic itself. For example, when Dushassan attempts to disrobe Draupadi, she invokes the help of Krishna of Dwarka, Krishna the loved one of the gops and gopis. It needs to be recalled that Draupadi was a great devotee of Krishna and was familiar with Krishna's love for the cowherd maidens of Braj. In brief one could state that Krishna is one, but is perceived in many different forms through the eye of the devotee. He is the one who stays in Golok, He is Narain of Vaikunth, He is Mahavishnu, He is the divine mischievous child of Vrindavan and Braj and the diplomat Yogeshwar of Mahabharat. The camera for the purpose of this book attempts to portray the child Krishna as known and remembered in Braj and more so in Vrindavan.

Kurukshetra, which historically was the scene of the epic battle of the Mahabharat, is at present in the state of Haryana — 150 km from Delhi. In the Chandogya Upanishad there is a mention of Krishna, son of Devaki and also of King Dhritrashtra, son of Vichitravirya.[17] Since both names are also mentioned in the epic Mahabharat, it may be said that both were contemporaries who lived at the same time, as historical characters, in the distant past in India. In the Mahabharat, Krishna is seen both as a historical character and also as an Avatar, when he reveals his true identity to Arjun by bestowing on him the power to see beyond the mortal world. The camera, not being blessed with this 'third eye' vision, has only captured pictorially all those places which from time immemorial have been associated with the Krishna leela and which continue to enrapture the devotees of Krishna.

The most widely accepted images of Krishna, which appear in the Harivansh Purana, are those of the playful Krishna of Braj surrounded by gops and gopis, indulging in childish mirth; the astute regent of Dwarka whose role in the Mahabharat saga is that of a seasoned diplomat and the upholder of women's honour, and of justice; and finally the supreme Godhead who, in the Bhagvat Gita, provides Arjun with the moral philosophy and spiritual strength for waging, what seems, a futile war. In all the three roles Krishna wields considerable supernatural powers which, while establishing his divinity, also raise him to a heightened position in popular imagination.

There are endless examples of these supernatural powers.

To cite a few of them, he kills Putna, when only at the tender age of a few months, by suckling at her breast until she dies; he tears apart Bakasur with his naked hands; Kesi, the demon with a horse's face, is suffocated to death when Krishna plunges his hand into his mouth; he retains the mood of playfulness and serenity after Kalia Nag is overpowered; the hurricane created by Tarnavrat is stopped by

11

12

11. Gokarneshwar: an incarnation of Shiva protecting the northern end of Mathura.

12. Rangeshwar: an incarnation of Shiva protecting the southern end of Mathura.

Krishna. Govardhan is lifted by Krishna at the tender age of seven, on his little finger, for seven days to protect the people of Braj; and even mother Yashoda, who constantly chastises the mischievous child Krishna, is dumbfounded when she is made to perceive the entire universe in the mouth of Krishna.[18] The creation of Mansiganga at Govardhan, the introduction of the festival of Annakut, the appearance of Radhakund and Shyamkund are just a few more examples from the Krishna legend to demonstrate the divine powers of Shri Krishna.[19]

The overriding picture of Krishna of Braj is as the embodiment of love, romance, serenity and devotion. This is the Krishna of the poets, the literary giants and also the sages of a later period. The stories of the child and the lover Krishna, spread to various parts of India and are immortalised in the poems of Surdas, Raskhan, Rahim, Bihari, Jaidev and many others. The main theme of the miniature paintings from up north in Kangra to mid-west in Rajasthan also depict the episodes related to the life and romantic exploits of Radha and Krishna. These paintings present the many-faceted Krishna, as the Godhead, the adorable child and the celestial lover.

The divine aspect of Krishna as described in the scriptures took a new dimension with the devotional poets' interpretation of the form and life-style of the deity. The poets, mostly of the sixteenth century, composed verses to describe the child Krishna, with his innocent, bewitching smile and his playful moods. Many of them composed poems adoring the flute and the charm of its music which is said to have enraptured the gops and gopis.

Krishna's powers as a dancer and a musician add yet another dimension to the great impact he had on his devotees, many of whom, like Hitharivansh, professed to have experienced divine instructions from Krishna, through dreams, to spread his message of love through music and dance forms. The development of the art of *ras* is again stated to be the result of such divine advice by Krishna to Ghamand Devji.

The description of Krishna, specially in the context of his stay in Braj, would not be complete without a mention of Shri Radha who, with Krishna, represented the much adulated divine couple. It has been said earlier that the image of Krishna as projected during his stay in Braj is one of love. The supreme manifestation of this love in a visible form is provided by Radha, in the presence of Krishna. According to Shri Aurobindo, "Radha is the personification of the absolute love for the Divine, total and integral in all parts of the being from the highest spiritual to the physical, bringing the absolute self-giving and total

13

15

13. Kansvadh. Malwa, circa AD 1660. Courtesy: National Museum, New Delhi.

14. Yamunaji: the river considered holy next to the Ganges. A number of episodes in Krishna's life are associated with Yamuna.

15. Yamuna Arti. Every morning and evening, the priest raises the brass lamp to move it in a ritual circular motion as a mark of respect to mother Yamuna, the consort of Krishna.

consecration of all the being and calling down into the body and the most material nature the supreme *Anand.*"[20] Shri Radha was supposed to have reflected the divine energy of Krishna. Ideologically, Radha and Krishna were, fundamentally, the same, like the two crests of the same wave, but for purposes of divine sport, they were located in two separate and yet inseparable bodies. The places associated with the Krishna legend are replete with stories depicting one of the two principal aspects of Krishna of Braj: his supernatural powers vis-a-vis demons and his romantic dalliance with Radha. This is manifested in

16. Idols of Yamuna and Krishna. Yamuna is also venerated as a consort of Krishna.

17. Wall painting at Kusumsarovar. The painting depicts episodes from Krishna's life. From inside the wall of Chhatri of Raja Surajmal of Bharatpur — 1764 AD.

18. Ek Pran Do Deh, Radha Krishna Temple, Nandgaon. The idol represents unity of the Divinity in love.

the descriptions associated with Giriraj Govardhan, Radhakund and, most of all, Vrindavan, the abode of Shri Vrinda (another name of Radha). The popular adoration of the divine couple Radha-Krishna continues to pervade the atmosphere of Braj land. Thus with a few exceptions, almost all the temples of Braj have an idol of Shri Radha or, failing that, a *Yantra* portraying Shri Radha, which is kept near the idol of Shri Krishna in the famous temples, such as in Bihariji, Radha Raman, Govindji and others.[21]

Places and Temples

स्वागत करते हैं
आज के पावन पर्व पर
युवा परिषद
हार्दिक स्वागत करता है।

The task of covering all the important landmarks associated with the Krishna legend in the land of Braj proved to be a stupendous one, especially since Krishna devotees tend to ascribe a sense of divinity even to the sand particles of the region suggesting that the black particles represented Krishna and the white, Radha. In my photographic coverage of the land of Braj I have allowed myself to be restricted only by the logistics of publication requirements and, of course, the limitations of the camera.

The camera follows the route generally taken by pilgrims as they walk, mostly barefooted, through the land of Braj.

I start from the nucleus of the land of Braj, that is, Mathura, which is situated on the highway called Shershah Suri Marg, about 154 km from Delhi. As one approaches Mathura, from a distance of about 6-8 km, one can see the flame-shaped dome of the Janmabhumi temple or the marble pavilion (birth-place of Shri Krishna) against the backdrop of the three domes of a mosque. The temple complex described as the Janmabhumi marks the place where Krishna, the eighth son of Vasudev and Devaki, is said to have been born in prison on the eighth day of the waning moon in the month of Bhadrapad (August-September) in Dwaparyug[22] (5000 B.C.). The base of the mosque was, according to the foreign traveller Tavernier,[23] once the plinth of the temple of Keshav Dev, reputed to be a most imposing temple until it was destroyed by Aurangzeb to be replaced by the mosque as it exists today. The underground cellar behind the marble pavilion is an old construction and is stated to be the prison cell where Devaki was imprisoned at the time of the birth of Krishna.

Near the Janmabhumi on the western side is a quadrangular tank of solid masonry. It is called Potrakund because supposedly Krishna's diapers were washed in this tank.

19. Sunset, Kusumsarovar. This place was a rendezvous of Radha and Krishna. (On page 41)

20. Vishram Ghat, another view.

21. Covered pathway to Vishram Ghat: a holy spot on the banks of the Yamuna.

22. Vishram Ghat. According to the legend, Krishna and Balram rested at this place after killing Kans, the tyrant ruler of Mathura.

23. Dwarkadheesh Temple. Built in 1871, it is the most venerated temple of Mathura.

There are four temples of Shiva on the four sides of Mathura: Bhuteshwar which is not far away from Janmabhumi on the western side, Pingleshwar on the east, Rangeshwar on the south and Gokaran Nath on the north. The last-mentioned is a seated figure of a giant with enormous eyes, long hair, beard and moustache. The presence of Shiva temples on the four sides of Mathura has earned Shiva the nickname of watchman of Mathura. Mathura was not only the city of the most magnificent Vaishnav temples but also Jain temples and Buddha Viharas. The frequent Muslim conquests of the region, starting at the time of Mahmud Ghaznavi and continuing until the time of Aurangzeb,[24] subjected the city to constant ravages. The present generation of temples was probably constructed on a low profile so as to minimise their attraction to invaders. Most of the temples that are famous in Mathura, as elsewhere in Braj, are associated with Krishna as the presiding deity, and are often associated with a supernatural phenomenon.

Dwarkadheesh is the most important temple in Mathura. (The literal meaning would be the Lord of Dwarka.) The temple is not only the oldest but also the most venerated of all the temples in Mathura.

The temple was founded in 1815 by Gokulpati Singh, a treasurer in the court of Scindias of Gwalior. It is approached by a richly carved gateway with a steep flight of steps opening onto a square courtyard. The main temple has a large covered courtyard, with walls painted with episodes from Krishna's life. The sanctum sanctorum of the temple is covered by a half-curved dome, more like the ceiling of an oriental palace.[25]

The inner courtyard of the temple has paintings of Dwarkadheesh and Krishna Leela painted at various places. Some of the popular ones show Krishna sitting in front of Surdas listening to his poetry, Krishna as the two-body-one-soul motif, depicting the concept of divine love between Radha and Krishna and Krishna as Dwarkadheesh. The temple is dedicated to the followers of Vallabhacharya *Pushtisampradaya* (sect) who continue to be administrators of the temple.

Vishramghat: Walking down to the Yamuna river, the most important place is Vishramghat, so named because Krishna and Balram rested here, after slaying King Kans and his wrestlers.[26]

The archway at Vishramghat is the place where the *Arti* of the River Yamuna is performed in the early morning and in the evening. Under the arch, the rulers of Benares and Datia were weighed against precious metals which were then given away in charity. Besides the Vishramghat, the river-bank for about three kilometres is studded with

23

24. Govardhan. The hilly range of Govardhan is considered the most sacred range in India. The episode of Krishna lifting the mountain range on his little finger is related to Govardhan.

25. Mansiganga. Govardhan. Krishna is stated to have invoked the Ganges to fill the pond at this spot. The place is considered so sacred that bathing in Mansiganga is equivalent to a holy dip in all sacred places of pilgrimage in India.

26. The monuments on the western bank of Kusumsarovar built for Raja Surajmal and his two wives.

24

ghats that have been demolished and reconstructed several times. An important landmark is the slender tower on the right side of the Vishramghat. This is called Satiburj.[27] The tower, originally of a much greater height, was partially damaged during the reign of Aurangzeb. On the whole, a walk along the Yamuna takes one through one of the most picturesque areas in Mathura which still has the flavour of medieval times.

There are several temples in this area, which have been erected over the last 200 years and belong to different sects. The outstanding ones are the temples of Kankali Devi, Mahavidya Devi, and the Ramji temple with the footprints of Dhruv, stated to have been installed by Bajranabh.

25

26

27. The idol of Udhav in the Udhav Temple at the far end of Kusumsarovar, dedicated to the messenger-cum-devotee of Lord Krishna. Udhav is best remembered for his dialogues with gopis while consoling them after they had been separated from Shri Krishna.

Madhuvan: About 10 km south-west of Mathura, we come to Madhuvan, which serves as a link between the times of Shri Ram of the Tretayug and Shri Krishna of the Dwaparyug. The town of Madhupur was supposedly established by Shatrughan (brother of Shri Ram) after killing the demon Madhu.[28] Later on Madhupur changed its name to Mathura and shifted towards the river-bank where it exists today. The place is also famous for the spot where Dhruv meditated at the age of five years and was rewarded with divine blessings. For his unswerving devotion, Dhruv was to be remembered as the steadfast northern polar star which provides direction to travellers on land and sea.

Govardhan: About 20 km west of Madhuvan is Govardhan. The name has been made familiar by paintings and sculptures depicting Krishna lifting the pyramidal hill on his little finger. In real life, Govardhan with a 22 km circumference is a hilly range running in a south easterly direction. A winding road encircles Govardhan and is the favoured route of countless devotees who annually perform the *parikrama* (circumambulation) of Govardhan. The 22 km hilly range has been traditionally venerated by millions of devotees from all over the country. So profound is the belief that no piece of stone is removed from the range. According to Adivarah Purana, even the mere touch of Govardhan would help atone the worst of sins, thus enabling a person to attain salvation.

Mythologically the homage and veneration shown to Govardhan appears to be for three main reasons:

One, Krishna very explicitly states that he is Giriraj, thus projecting a hill as symbolic of not only his best creation but himself and as such, turning it into an object of veneration. According to the scriptures, Shri Radha had requested Krishna to create a land of natural splendour where they could meet. Krishna granted the wish and Giriraj appeared from the chest of the Lord and descended on the earth. The holy mount was brought to Braj through the efforts of Maharishi Pulatsya.[29]

Two, Krishna lifts Giriraj for seven days on his little finger. By doing so, he protected the gops and gopis from the wrath of Lord Indra, who had instructed the clouds to rain for seven days incessantly so as to devastate the land. Ultimately, Indra realised the power of Shri Krishna and came down, riding on his elephant Airavat, to seek Krishna's pardon. The devotees point out a stone which has marks like an elephant's footprint. It is there that Airavat descended and knelt for Indra to alight and seek pardon from Krishna.[30]

Third, the entire range of Govardhan hills has provided an idyllic setting for the play of gops and gopis and Shri Radha-Krishna meetings. Two rocks, one with vermilion powder and the other with Kohl powder (*kajal*), are said to represent the frolics of Krishna with Shri Radha in the caves of Giriraj. The Puranic description of Govardhan extols the natural splendour of its forests, the trees laden with fruits, the variety of flowers, its caves and ponds. The rocky formations of Govardhan hills change their colour from greyish blue to coppery red,

28. Radhakund and Shyamkund. Both the water reservoirs are said to have been created by Shri Radha and Krishna. The water in both is provided from the holy places in all parts of India.

depending on the time of the day. The stones also present different pictures in the 22 km long formation. At places they appear like slates, mounted one over the other, at others they are boulders or rounded small stones. However, the landscape is changing and it remains a barren stretch for most of the year. Some even claim that Giriraj is shrinking in size. The fact however remains that the landmarks associated with episodes of Krishna's life, in and around Giriraj, are in a gross state of neglect and disrepair.

In the more recent past, the hilly ranges have provided shelter for devotees of different sects who have stayed and meditated in the hope of being graced by a vision of Shri Krishna. Such a favour, bestowed by Shri Krishna, has been claimed by a number of devotees such as Shri Chaitanya Mahaprabhu, Sanatan Goswami, Shri Vallabhacharya, Surdas, Shri Krishna Das and many others.

29. Radhakund — eastern end. The samadhi of Raghunath Das can be seen in the distance.

There are several places in and around Giriraj that catch the eye of the camera. Hence selecting the important ones, we start with Mansiganga.

Mansiganga: It is essentially a water reservoir extending over a large area and projecting out on the north-western end, giving the impression that it was a river. It is surrounded on all sides by bathing ghats. On the whole, the scene is reminiscent of any Hindu religious centre by a riverside. It is most picturesque from the western end, against the backdrop of the royal pavilions of the house of Bharatpur. The temple of Giriraj is under renovation at present. When completed it would be the centrepiece of attraction clearly visible from anywhere around Mansiganga.

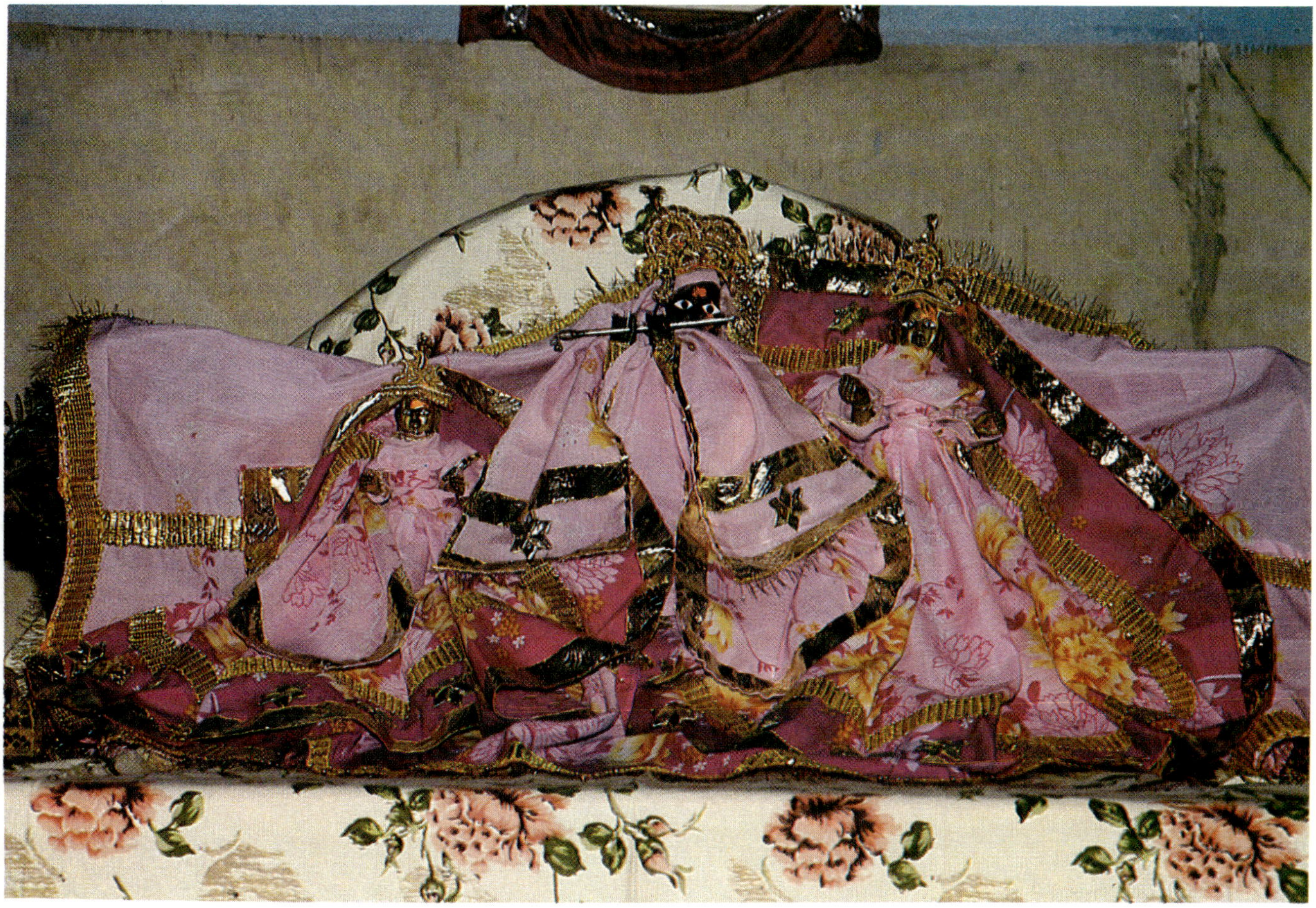

31

The origin of Mansiganga is linked with the legend of the killing of Vrashmasur.[31] It is stated that Shri Radha and others had asked Krishna to atone for his sin of killing Vrashmasur. Shri Krishna invoked the Ganges to appear and form Mansiganga as it exists today. He bathed in this tank to purify himself. Later on this water reservoir was also used by the divine couple for water sports. The Gargasamhita gives great importance to a bath in Mansiganga as a ritual for self-purification.[32] In the sixteenth century, Raja Mansingh of Jaipur provided the stonework for the steps around Mansiganga. The people living around Mansiganga claim to have witnessed some strange sights. For example, very often the people report seeing a streak of milk sprouting out of the water surface which stays for a few hours before it disappears.

A vault-like red sandstone building on the northern end of Mansiganga is the temple of Hari Dev built by Raja Bhagwandas of Amber.[33] Clustered amongst big and small modern buildings, it still presents a facade of an extremely massive and imposing structure. One has to visualise its full glory when it was mounted with two *shikhars* (pinnacles) over the sanctum; these were levelled during the period of upheavals in Braj. The old statue of Hari Dev is stated to have been installed during the time of Bajranabh.[34]

30. Lalitaji Temple, Uncha Gaon. Shri Lalita, one of the eight companions of Shri Radha, was also married to Shri Krishna.

31. The temple with the idol of Shri Lalita and Krishna by her side.

Moving out from Govardhan, one passes by Danghati. At this point the road passes through a narrow opening in the Giriraj range. Krishna and gops, it is said, would block the opening, thereby preventing the gopis from carrying milk and milk products to Mathura, the capital city of Kans. They would assert their own rights to use the butter and milk as they wished. Hence the name, which literally means the valley of donations or Danghati. The next spot to be covered is Jatipura, about 5 km from Danghati. Shri Vallabhacharya had constructed a temple devoted to Shri Nathji on top of the hill. There is an interesting story that a cowherd, who used to take a Brahmin's cow for grazing on the hills, noted that the cow visited a certain spot and discharged her milk. The unbelievable statement of the cowherd was later confirmed by Vallabhacharya. On removing the stones from the site, the idol was revealed. This was addressed as Shri Nathji by the Acharya.[35] During Aurangzeb's reign, the idol of Shri Nathji was removed to Nathdwara in Udaipur where it continues to be under the care of Vallabhsampradaya. Remnants of the large temple complex that was built by Vallabhacharya can still be seen on top of the hill.

Kusumsarovar: On the road from Govardhan to Radhakund, the skyline presents a breathtaking landscape. The place had been the chosen spot of Shri Radha for collecting flowers and performing *ras.* Hence the name Kusumsarovar.[36] Later on, it was selected by Bajranabh, to arrange for a reading of the Shrimad Bhagvat so that Shri Krishna could be recalled in person, to help identify the important places of his times. At present the 130 sq metres of artificial lake on its western side is occupied by the pavilions of the house of Bharatpur. The main and the most imposing one is that of Raja Surajmal, the founder of the Bharatpur dynasty. It is flanked on either side by two smaller pavilions, almost identical in shape, belonging to Rani Hansiya and Rani Kishori, the two queens of Raja Surajmal.[37] The canopy over the main pavilion has paintings depicting episodes of the life of Krishna as also of Raja Surajmal in court. In spite of poor maintenance, the paintings have still managed to retain their original colour and beauty.

On the left of the pavilion on the Kusumsarovar is the temple dedicated to Udhav, who had apparently preferred to stay in this place in the form of shrubs and creepers, so that he would be in touch with the holy dust of Braj and Vrindavan.

Nearby is also another place, the samadhi of Shri Narayan Swami, whose devotional songs and *rasleela* attracted the attention of Shri Krishna himself.

Radhakund and Shyamkund: Near Kusumsarovar are two ponds, both of which are amongst many such places rediscovered by Shri Chaitanya. The two ponds were referred to as Gauri and Kali lakes[38] until Shri Chaitanya expounded their origin referring to episodes from the life of Radha and Krishna. The story concerns the killing of Arishtasur (demon with bull's head) by Shri Krishna. Kans apparently knew that the places in and around Govardhan served as a rendezvous for the divine lovers. He chose Arishtasur, the demon with the strength of a bull, to kill Krishna. Krishna was performing *ras* with Radha and the gopis when Arishtasur attacked them with the fury of a hurricane. Yet with lightning speed Krishna tackled Arishtasur, holding him by the horns, pulling them out and then killing the bull.

Although much relieved, Shri Radha pointed out to Krishna that the demon had a bull's head and since the slaying of the cow or the bull was a sin, Krishna had to perform penance by bathing in the holy *tirthas* (places of pilgrimage).

32. Premsarovar, Barsana. The origin of the sarovar is related to tears shed at this spot by Shri Radha and Krishna.

33. Asheshwar Mahadev: an old temple dedicated to Shiva at Nandgaon.

34. Nandgaon Temple, dedicated to Nandbaba, his wife Yashoda and their two sons, Krishna and Balram. The Nand family and clan had shifted to this place from Gokul and hence the name.

33

Krishna responded by digging a pond with the pressure of his heel. All the tirthas appeared in person to pour water in the pond which was then described as Shyamkund.[39] Although Krishna dutifully bathed to wash away his sins, he insisted that Radha and others had also to atone for their sins, as they had witnessed the killing of Arishtasur.

Shri Radha created another pond by scratching the earth with a broken bangle. All the tirthas again appeared in person and requested Shri Radha to let them fill it with water so that she could purify herself. The pond was then named Radhakund. Both the ponds match each other for the sanctity associated with them.

34

The twin ponds are surrounded by temples, meditation huts and *samadhis* of saints of yester years. Of special mention are the samadhis of Raghunath Bhatt Goswami, Krishnadaskaviraj Goswami (responsible for compilation of the book *Chaitanya Charitramrit*) and Raghunath Das Goswami. All these three devotees are stated to have left this world on the 12th day of the receding moon in the month of *Kartik*, though in different years. Shri Raghunath Das Goswami, a disciple of Shri Chaitanya, apparently rediscovered these two ponds which had almost physically disappeared at that time. He had a vision of the five Pandavas existing as five peepal trees, at the northern end of Shyamkund. It was therefore decided not to cut down these trees, thereby giving the northern end of Shyamkund an irregular shape. Amongst the temples one is the temple of the tongue of Govardhan. The story goes that Shri Raghunath Das Goswami wished a well dug in the temple, and that a labourer while digging it struck a stone which showed signs of bleeding. That very night, the Goswami supposedly had a dream indicating that the bleeding piece of stone was the tongue of Giriraj. It was then installed at the place where it exists today.

35. Shriji Temple, Barsana. Dedicated to Shri Radha, the temple is located on a high peak called Brahma Peak.

From Govardhan to Barsana is a distance of 12 km on a metalled road, passing through green fields and clusters of villages. Barsana was the home of Shriji or Shri Radha. According to a popular saying, Krishna considered only four places in Braj as his home, these being Vrindavan, Madhupuri (Mathura), Barsana and Nandgaon. Very little seems to be known about Shri Radha. Even what is known is tainted and malicious hearsay, not based on the scriptures. Shri Radha, on a supramental plane, is the most intimate part of Krishna, often picturised as one soul

and two bodies. On a descriptive plane, the creative aspect of cosmic intelligence in Shri Krishna and Shri Radha is the source of energy. Mythologically Shri Radha or *Ladliji* was only nine months elder to Krishna to whom she was married. The marriage of the celestial couple was performed in their infancy by Lord Brahma in Bhandirvan.[40]

It is an exhilarating sight to watch the contours of the temple of *Ladliji* (Radha) as one nears Barsana. The temple located on the Brahma hill can be seen from a distance of about 2 km. The hill has

36. Ghevar Van: the forest at the back of Shriji Temple.

37. Sankrikhor. The name refers to the narrow passage in the hills stated to be in the area where Krishna and other gopes would collect tax in the form of milk and milk products.

38. Shri Radha collecting flowers. A painting inside the hall of Shriji Temple, Barsana.

36

four branches like the four faces of Brahma. The four important buildings on the premises are Shri Radha temple, Manmandir, Dangarh and Morkuti. Each one of these is associated with stories from the Radha and Krishna leela. For example, at Dangarh Radha pretends to be angry with Krishna who in turn implores Radha to forgive him. The temple devoted to Shri Radha is located on the highest point of the hill overlooking the plains.

Almost all the temples were built around the 19th century.[41] Another magnificent temple on Brahma hill was built by the Jaipur rulers. It is well maintained and provides a commanding view of Ghevarvan, a holy van (forest). Morkuti located on the hill top a little

further away was apparently the spot where Krishna, dressed in peacock feathers, danced to please Radha, who excitedly exclaimed "*mor*" which in local dialect means peacock and also means mine, that is, 'belonging to me'. A small temple has been constructed recently on the hill top to mark the celestial spot.

The largest temple, which is the most recently built, is currently the seat for the enthronement of the deity, Shri Radha. A long flight of steps from the road leads to the temple and the main courtyard. During special celebrations like the birthday of Ladliji or the Holi festival, the courtyard presents some of the most riotous scenes of ecstasy.

39. Matki Leela, a painting portraying Krishna breaking an earthern milk pot of a gopi.

40

41

40. Chaurasi Khamba, said to be a part of an old temple at Kamvan. Each pillar carving represents a variety of species of life found on earth.

41. Stone pillar carving, Chaurasi Khamba.

Sankrikhor:[42] This is a narrow passage between two natural parts of Brahma hills. Beyond it is Ghevarvan, which used to be a dense forest and a favourite place for the sporting *leela* of Radha and Krishna. In the not-too-distant past, a devotee named Shri Kishori Ali had claimed to have had the personal vision of Kishoriji (Radha) in this *van*. The samadhi of this devotee is located near Shri Krishnakund in Ghevarvan. The *van* continues to attract sadhus and devotees, committed to the worship of Shriji (Radha).

Pilipokhar:[43] Situated at the north-western end of Barsana, is the largest pond surrounded by Pilu trees. The place was a favourite spot of Shri Radha whenever she wanted to seek solitude. The name Pilipokhar or yellow pond is attributed to the legend in which the water of the lake is claimed to have turned yellow, after Radha, who used yellow sandalwood paste, had taken a bath in the pond.

Premsarovar:[44] About 6 km from Barsana is the pond where Krishna, Radha and the gopis had indulged in a variety of playful sports. The tank is provided with flights of steps all round and is surrounded by green trees on all sides. Being not much frequented by visitors, it is a suitable place for meditation.

From the courtyard of the temple at Barsana on a clear day one can see Unchagaon, the birth-place of Shri Lalitaji, a very close associate of Shri Radha. Unchagaon has a small but beautiful temple on the hill top to commemorate the birth-place of Shri Lalitaji. Below the temple is the samadhi of Shri Narayan Bhatt, a devotee of Shri Radha.[45] Shri Narayan Bhatt was a prolific writer and his works, totalling sixty, included *Braj Bhakti Vilas* and *Bhaktiras Tarangini.*

Nandgaon: This place is about 6 km from Barsana and is located on a hill associated by legend with Shiva. In view of the special relationship between the celestial couple, Radha and Krishna, these two villages too acquired a special significance which is locally respected even today. Thus, a male visitor from Nandgaon to Barsana, it is claimed, can walk into any household and would be accorded the courtesy due to a son-in-law.

Temple of Nandbaba: The temple dedicated to Nandbaba on top of the hill, with its two towers (shikhars), commands a view of the Mathura valley. One has to climb a winding narrow passage of 116 steps to reach the main entrance to the temple. The temple built in a style not seen in Vrindavan and Barsana is not more than two hundred years old. However, the icons of Krishna and Balram are stated to be very old. The images of Nand and Yashoda are of more recent origin. The temple has a large open nave used by the devotees for group singing or studying religious books. On the whole, the rustling wind, the sandalwood incense scented air, the occasional ringing of the bells, provide an atmosphere of serenity and devotion.

Nandeshwar: The courtyard of the temple has an important and old shrine, that of Nandeshwar. It is said that Lord Shiva wanted to see the infant Krishna. However, mother Yashoda got a shock, seeing Shiva's face covered with ashes and snakes encircling his neck. She did not comply with the wishes of Shiva, stating that the child Krishna

42. Birth of Krishna. Vasudeva crossing the Yamuna carrying infant Krishna from Mathura to Gokul. Early 17th century painting from National Museum, New Delhi.

43. Vrinda Devi, the idol of Vrindavan's presiding deity, installed in Radha Govind Temple, Kamvan, at the time of Mughal invasion of Vrindavan.

43

would be frightened on seeing him. Shiva left the place without seeing Krishna. However, the legend goes that as soon as Shiva left, the child Krishna started crying and stopped crying only when Shiva was recalled. The child smiled at Shiva. The grateful Yashoda asked Shiva what she could do for him. Shiva asked permission to stay in the same precincts and eat part of the food left over by Krishna. The *Shivaling* within the temple is stated to have been installed by Bajranabh and is offered the remains of the food served to the deity Krishna in the main temple.[46]

44. Thakurani Ghat — the place where Krishna was brought from Mathura to Gokul.

45. Brahmand Ghat, Gokul, Mahavan: the place where Krishna showed the universe (Brahmand) in his mouth when prevented by Yashoda from eating mud.

49

50

46. Mud cakes, Brahmand Ghat, symbolizing mud eaten by Krishna.

47. Figure of Baldev, Dauji Temple

48. Mansukha: a playmate of Shri Krishna.

49. Dauji Temple. The largest idol of Balram is said to have been installed here by Bajranabh.

50. Raval Temple: the place where Brishbhan found Shri Radha lying on a lotus in a pond.

Just outside the outer courtyard of the main Nandbaba temple, there are many idols of Krishna, installed over a period of time, one of the oldest being that of Yashodanandan and another unique one, in front of the northern entrance of the main temple, is of Radha-Krishna symbolising two bodies and one soul.

On a clear day, standing on the towers of the main temple, one can see some other important places associated with the Krishna *leela*, the most significant being the following:

Pavansarovar: As the name indicates, Krishna may have brought his herd of cows to drink water here. It must have been a beautiful lake with well laid-out ghats, now in a state of neglect. It is supposed to be one of the four largest lakes in Braj. The other three are Chandsarovar at Parsoli near Govardhan, Premsarovar at Ghazipur near Barsana and Mansarovar across Yamuna near Mat.

51. Krishna playing flute. Malwa, circa AD 1661. Courtesy: National Museum, New Delhi.

52. A devotional singer at Gokul.

52

Shri Sanatan Goswami, a devotee of Krishna and follower of Shri Chaitanya, had his meditation cottage on the bank of Pavansarovar. It is said that Sanatan Goswami was so absorbed in his devotional thought that he neglected to eat and Krishna himself appeared in front of him to serve food. Later when Sanatan Goswami realised the divine presence, he felt blessed.

Terkadamb: At a stone's throw from Nandgaon, on the northern side, is a grove of Kadamb trees, where Krishna used to rest before collecting the cows to return to Nandgaon in the evening. The place was also a chosen spot of Roop Goswami for meditation.

53

53. Govind Dev Temple, Vrindavan. It was built in 1647 AD by Swai Raja Man Singh under the direction of Rup and Sanatan Goswami and is considered to be the most impressive edifice of a Hindu temple in North India.

54. Entrance to Govind Dev Temple.

54

55

56

Udhavkyari: After leaving Vrindavan, Krishna sent his messenger Udhav to pacify the gopis who were heart-broken by their separation from him. Udhav returned to Lord Krishna and narrated the unending love for Krishna expressed by the gopis. This meeting took place at the spot now described as Udhavkyari,[47] which is considered a very pious spot by the devotees.

Celestial footprints: The child Krishna supposedly left his footprints in Nandgaon on the stones, which would withstand the passage of time. It is stated in Shrimad Bhagvat that Akrur, the chariot driver of Kans, saw these footprints when he came to fetch Krishna and Balram.

55. Sanctum sanctorum, Govind Dev Temple, with delicate stonework.

56. The idol of Govind Devji. The original idol was shifted to Jaipur during Mughal invasions.

57. Devotees inside Bihariji Temple, Vrindavan.

Kamvan: About 8 km north of Nandgaon is Kamvan, one of the oldest and very famous places of pilgrimage. Kamvan has been described as the place where the wishes of mortals would always be fulfilled. It was the playground of the celestial lovers and their playmates. It is also described as old Vrindavan as the idol of Shri Vrinda when brought out of Vrindavan had been installed in this village. Mythologically the place also finds a mention in the Mahabharat, as being the location where the five Pandava brothers spent their year of exile in disguise.

Vimalkund: Approaching from Nandgaon, one passes by Vimalkund, on the south-west end of the township. At this spot Krishna had apparently performed *ras* with the many daughters of Vimal Raj, the king of Sindh (now in Pakistan). They found the fulfilment of their life-long desire to be with Krishna, hence the name Vimalkund. To devotees, one dip in the Vimalkund is equivalent to having at least seven dips in holy Pushkar. All round the tank are small temples devoted to various gods and goddesses. The place is also important for *tantric* worship.

Kameshwarmahadev Temple: A little beyond Vimalkund on the western side is the temple of Kameshwarmahadev, considered as one of the oldest Shiva temples. The *Shivaling* here is stated to have been installed by Bajranabh.

The other important temples of historic importance are of Vrinda-devi, Gokulchandramaji and Madan Mohan. The idols from the last two were removed from Braj to Bikaner during the period of Mughal repression. They were later installed at the present-day temples at Kamvan.

57

The idol of Vrindadevi, the presiding deity of Vrindavan, was installed at the Radha-Govind temple. According to a popular anecdote, the idol of Vrinda, along with others, was being removed from Vrindavan to a place of safety.[48] The chariot carrying the idol of Vrindadevi stopped on reaching Kamvan. No efforts to move the chariot proved effective. Hence Vrindadevi's idol was installed at Kamvan, which was also the geographical boundary of Vrindavan.

Chaurasikhamba[49] (Eighty-four Pillars): Moving through the Kamvan township one can find evidence of a prosperous era — the ruins of grand oriental buildings, palaces and temples. Further north in the Kamvan is the temple of Chaurasikhamba. It is interesting to note that Kamvan is associated with the number 84. This includes 84 pillars of the temple, 84 temples and 84 places of pilgrimage. The carvings on the pillars in the temple at Kamvan are reminiscent of similar carvings in the Nandbhavan at Mahavan.

59

60

58. Monkeys at play in the courtyard of Govind Dev Temple.

59. Tulsi Pujan. Tulsi, also known as Vrinda, is revered in Braj.

60. Thakur: Madan Mohan of Shri Krishna Chaitanya Bhattji Temple, Vrindavan.

61

61. Jugal Kishore Temple, Vrindavan (1627 AD). An interesting part is the arch with relief work showing Krishna lifting the Govardhan hill.

62. Choir arch with Govardhan Leela, Jugal Kishore Temple, Vrindavan.

63. Madan Mohan Temple, Vrindavan. An 'L' shaped architecture of the temple built in the same period as Govind Dev temple. The tower on the chapel is richly covered with sculptured panels. The text provides the unusual story about the construction of the temple.

62

63

Moving out of the Kamvan township, one comes across several minor places which carry references to the Krishna legend, such as Charanpahari,[50] situated on the hill top with the footprint marks of Shri Krishna, or Bhojanthali, the place where Krishna shared food with his playmates in the jungle, or the Lukluk Kund where he indulged in the sport of hide-and-seek.

Gokul and Mahavan, though separated from each other by 5 km, are often mentioned as almost indistinguishable from each other. Gokul in a generic sense means a place where the gops live. But mythologically, the place is referred to as the abode of Nand, where infant Krishna was brought by Vasudev to the house of Nand.[51]

The present Gokul and Mahavan are a part of Vrindavan, which is in turn a part of Brajdham. The revival of the place is mainly due to the efforts of Mahaprabhu Vallabhacharya who had apparently been guided to this spot by a beautiful goddess, an incarnation of Shri Yamuna. The Thakuranighat established by Shri Vallabhacharya for meditation in time became an important religious centre for followers of Pushtimarg.

The house of Nandbaba situated on the banks of the Yamuna, where Balkrishna had been brought up by his foster parents, now houses a temple devoted to the family of Nand — Yashoda, Krishna and Balram. The original building with 84 pillars has several spots which are connected to episodes from Krishna's childhood *leela* such as the spot where Krishna was apparently tied to the stand of the grinding mortar for stealing butter, or the spot where Putna was killed by infant Krishna, or the place where Yogmaya, the infant girl exchanged with child Krishna and killed by Kans, was born.[52]

On the outskirts of the village is a small temple devoted to Shiva. The story is identical to what one hears at Nandgaon. It is said to be the spot where Shiva stayed on to worship Krishna, who had initially not been allowed to see Shiva lest he be upset by Shiva's awe-inspiring looks.

Brahmandghat: On the bank of the river Yamuna is located a spot associated with one of the most famous episodes in Krishna's childhood which figures in songs and poems of saints like Surdas. According to the story, on receiving a complaint that Krishna was seen eating mud from the banks of Yamuna, Yashoda bade her errant child Krishna to open his mouth, and was amazed to see the entire universe inside Krishna's mouth! This reconfirmed her thoughts that her Balgopal was no ordinary child. A small temple along the bank of Yamuna reminds visitors of the spot where this event supposedly took place.

64. Flower shops at Bihariji Temple.

65. Yogmaya Temple located in the left wing of Govind Dev Temple.

66

The other places of interest in the trans-Yamuna area include Dauji, Raval, Bhandirvan, and Mansarovar.

Dauji: The temple of Dauji (familiar form of address for Baldev) has a unique history. Apparently the idol installed by Bajranabh escaped the wrath of Aurangzeb's forces who, mysteriously, could not locate it.

Raval: Shri Radha revealed herself at this place as an infant to Brishbhan when he was returning from the temple. The place has also a small temple of Shri Radha Rani.

Bhandirvan: About 18 km away, near a small village is the well, where Brahma performed the marriage of Radha to Krishna. The small temple by the side of the well has an idol of Krishna applying vermilion to the forehead of Shri Radha. The Adivarah Purana and Gargasamhita

66. The painted deity of Bankebihariji, Swami Haridas's Ishtadev.

67. The place where the deity of Radha Raman was revealed in its existing form.

67

give a detailed account of the marriage, which took place without the knowledge of Nand or Brishbhan. Another episode associated with Bhandirvan is that Krishna had apparently thrust a stick in the ground to strike water which would quench the thirst of his gopis. The water of the well is stated to turn milky even today whenever the new moon happens to fall on a Monday.

Mansarovar: This is one of the four large lakes known for their beautiful natural setting. The lake, located about 2 km from Vrindavan across the Yamuna, was the preferred place of Shri Hitharivansh for meditation. Mythologically this lake got its name from Shri Radha's feeling hurt at Krishna's neglect, and his attempts to placate her.[53]

68. Radha Raman, Shri Gopal Bhatt's Ishtadev, manifested itself in 1542 from a spindle-shaped black stone (saligram). This is the smallest of the deities in Vrindavan.

There is a temple dedicated to Shri Radha on the banks of the lake. Also, nearby are the huts of Shri Vallabhacharya and Shri Vitthalnath.

Vrindavan: The importance of Vrindavan as the sensitive heart of Braj has been stated earlier. Suffice it to say that it is the land of Vrinda (the other name of Shri Radha) who is also the presiding deity of Vrindavan. It may be recalled that Shri Radha did not leave Vrindavan, when Krishna left for Mathura and later on for Dwarka. The present Vrindavan is situated on the western bank of the river Yamuna, which almost surrounds the city in a semi-circular arch on three sides. Coming from Delhi, a small road near Chhatikra takes a left turn for Vrindavan which is 6.5 km from the turning. The other main road to Vrindavan is from Mathura.

Birla Temple: Coming out of Mathura on the Vrindavan road, is the imposing Birla Temple, a recent structure built by the industrial house of the Birlas. The architectural style attempts a combination of red sandstone and the deep yellow colour on the motifs and the railings. An important feature of the temple is the tall stone pillar on which are inscribed all the 18 chapters of Shrimad Bhagvat Gita.

Akrurji Ka Temple: Akrur, the charioteer of Kans, was sent to Nandbaba to fetch Krishna and Balram to Mathura. Akrur had stopped at this spot to rest a while. When Akrur stepped into the river for ablution, he was able to see Sheshashai Vishnu in the water of the Yamuna.[54] This made him confident of the victory of the celestial children he was carrying to the court of Kans.

Bhatrod Temple: Within a stone's throw from Akrur temple is the Bhatrod temple of Bihariji. In Shrimad Bhagvat, the place is identified with the episode where Krishna and his playmates were provided food by the wives of the Brahmins, when their husbands had refused to spare any food offerings for them.[55]

The entire road to Vrindavan from this point is lined with temples. Some of the important ones are on the left side of the road, such as the temple of Pagalbaba in white marble, and the Jaipur temple in pale sandstone. On the right side of the road is the temple of Rama Krishna Mission. Near the municipal barrier is the temple of *Gaudiasampradaya* (Gaudiamath) with five conical towers.

Vrindavan is reported to be a city of approximately five thousand temples. It would be difficult to cover all of these. Some of the important ones were constructed in the sixteenth century during the reign of Akbar. The temples built during this period set the pace for the revival of Krishnaism and the glory of Vrindavan.

70

Four temples of great distinction were built during this period. These include Govind Dev, Gopinath, Jugalkishore and Madan Mohan. The importance of these temples lies not only in the architectural style, but also the feeling of intense devotion that is felt for them.

Govind Dev temple situated on a high mound, not far from the bus stand in Vrindavan, is the largest and the most imposing. According to F.S. Growse, "It is the most impressive religious edifice which Hindu art has ever produced in Northern India."[56] These comments recorded more than a hundred years ago still hold good. Some people, mostly foreigners, compare the layout with a Greek cross.

The nave, formed of overlapping brackets with radiating arches, is located at the centre of the cross. The walls are ten feet thick, laced with red sandstone. The main entrance to the temple is from the eastern gate where one climbs five steps from the plinth to reach the main gate. On entering, one is struck by the vastness of the space, placement of pillars and arches reminiscent of similar work at Fatehpur Sikri. Passing the *sabha mandap* (nave), one sees a rich ornamental doorway that leads to another chamber, which connects the two lateral buildings. In front is the sacrarium which was destroyed during the later Mughal period and partially restored in the early part of this century.

69. Ashtasakhi Temple, Vrindavan. Built in 1889. the temple is dedicated to Shri Radha. Krishna and the eight companions of Shri Radha.

70. Krishna Balram Temple, Vrindavan.

71. Deity of Radha Krishna.
Krishna Balram Temple.

73

74

The entire exterior made of red sandstone gives out a radiant glow, when lit by the rays of the morning sun. The temple was originally located on the banks of a large tank, which has since been filled up for construction.

72. Rangji Temple. It was built by Seth Govind Das and Radha Kishan in 1851. The temple is dedicated to Rangji and is the leading temple of Ramanuj Sampradaya.

73. Gopuram of Rangji Temple, Vrindavan. This is the only temple in North India of South Indian style of architecture.

74. Garud Sthamba — the golden pillar. It is fifty feet high and about 24 ft underground inside the courtyard of Rangji Temple.

The idol of Govind Dev, which was installed in this temple, apparently revealed itself in a dream to Roop Goswami. The idol was excavated from the mound where the temple is now located. Later on, Savai Raja Mansingh of Jaipur undertook to construct the building as it exists today. The engravings in stone on the north side of the temple give the names of the artisan, the architect and the founder.

The idol of Gov nd Dev like many others was taken out of the temple to Jaipur in Aurangzeb's time where it continues to remain under the patronage of the house of Jaipur.[57] A replica of the idol was installed in the early British period and a new temple of Govindji was constructed just behind the old one.

75. Kesivadh by Shri Krishna. Malwa, 1680 AD. The horse-headed demon was killed by Krishna with bare hands at this place and hence the name. Courtesy: National Museum, New Delhi.

76. Kesighat, Vrindavan. The tall richly carved building in pale sandstone adds beauty to the ghat famous from the time of Krishna.

75

76

The idol of Shri Vrinda, now installed at Kamvan, was originally placed in the right wing of this temple. It was sent to Vrindavan from Jagannathpuri by the king of Puri. The basement on the left side of the lateral wing also houses the idol of Yogmaya. This was worshipped by Sanatan Goswami. It can be seen with the permission of the priest.

A seven-storey building with five minarets, surrounded by a large-sized tank, had been visualised in the original design of the temple. Even in its present diminutive form, the building radiates grace and dignity.

77. Kesighat: another view.

78. Kusum Sarovar, Govardhan.

Gopinath: The temple dating back to the same period as Govind Dev, or even earlier, was built by one of the chieftains of Raja Mansingh, the builder of the Govind Dev temple.[58] It is in a dilapidated condition with much of the original construction either destroyed or having fallen down. The temple was restored partly by a rich businessman of Bengal, Nand Kumar Ghose, who also helped in the construction of a new Madan Mohan temple.

Jugalkishore Temple: Built in red sandstone, the temple has a large nave about 7-1/2 metres square.[59] The entrance is from the door facing east. The main doorway has an interesting relief work of Krishna lifting Govardhan on his little finger.

Madan Mohan Temple:[60] It is located on a high mound near Kalia Mardan, another important spot associated with Krishna leela. The idol of Madan Mohan, which was installed, in the temple, was given to Sanatan Goswami, a disciple of Shri Chaitanya. It was installed at a place overlooking the river Yamuna. Its construction is attributed to an interesting episode. One day a merchant from Punjab was taking his sailing boat full of commercial goods to Agra. The boat got stuck near the ghat where Sanatan Goswami lived and would not move. After three days, the merchant became restive and asked for help. He was conducted by a small boy in the presence of Sanatan Goswami with the assurance that the saint would do the needful. The saint revealed that this was a divine design and that Krishna had taken the form of the boy. The merchant vowed to build a temple for Madan Mohan if his boat got released and he made a profit. The construction of the Madan Mohan temple indicates how well the wishes of the merchant must have been fulfilled.

The approach to the temple is through a flight of steps. The temple complex comprises a *mandap* (nave), *antardala* (choir) and *garbhagrah* (sacrarium). The temple is tower-shaped with a crown. The exterior is covered with elegantly sculptured panels.

Bankebihari Temple: The idol of Shri Bankebihari was revealed to Swami Haridas.[61] It is said that Haridas would pay obeisance to one particular spot in Nidhivan, before starting his day of singing and meditation. On persistent enquiries by his devotees as to the reason for his behaviour, he asked them to dig the place. A radiant light was noticed to emanate from an object. Thus was revealed the idol of Bihariji on the 5th day after the new moon in the month of February. The day is celebrated as Bihari Panchami in Vrindavan. Initially the idol was installed in Nidhivan. It was brought to the present site when the existing temple was completed in 1864 A.D. This temple attracts the largest number of devotees throughout the year. The service to

79. Sevakunj, the place believed to be visited by the Divinity every night. It was given prominence by Shri Hitharivanshji who constructed a temple dedicated to Shri Radha.

80

81

the Lord is also unique, as there is no *Arti* in the morning (Mangla Arti) as is the custom in other temples. It is believed that since Bihariji performed *ras* every night and retired late he woke up late too.

Radharaman Temple:[62] The temple, not too far away from Bihariji, and very near to Nidhivan, is well known for the anecdote about the miraculous revelation of the idol. It is said that Shri Gopal Bhatt, a devotee, had a black stone (shaped like Saligram) as the idol. He had an earnest desire to see the stone taking a form so that he could dress the adored deity as he wanted to. This miracle did happen. One fine day, he found the stone taking the shape of Radharaman, as is seen today. The idol is in black stone and is the smallest amongst the famous ones in the land of Braj. The samadhis of Shri Gopal Bhatt and other disciples are located behind the temple but within the same compound.

Ashtsakhi Temple:[63] Radha had an entourage of eight companions who represented the eight forms of Shakti with which she revealed herself on the earth. There is only one temple, built in 1928, dedicated to the eight companions of Shri Radha. The temple is of pale pink sandstone and located very near the old Madan Mohan temple. It attracts devotees mostly from eastern India.

Krishna Balram Temple:[64] This temple in white marble, built in 1975 A.D. by the International Society of Krishna's Consciousness (ISKCON), is located at Ramanreti in Vrindavan. The place was once a large tract of sand, and a favoured meeting place of Radha and Krishna. The temple was funded by donations from the followers of Shri A.C. Bhaktivedanta Swami Prabhupad, founder of ISKCON, who opened the temple in 1975. The three archways inside the temple have Shri Krishna Balram in the centre, Shri Gaur Nitai on the left and Radha Shyam Sunder on the right. The statue of Prabhupad located near the altar of Shri Gaur Nitai reflects a mood which is serene and sublime. The verandahs on the two sides have paintings depicting the life of Krishna. On the whole, the temple, though new, presents a highly vibrant atmosphere of devotion and grandeur.

Kesighat:[65] The left bank of Yamuna presents one of the most picturesque sights in the whole of Braj. Starting from the Madan Mohan temple to the Yamunaghat, is a stretch of ornamented buildings. These buildings made of pink and red sandstone were constructed by the princely houses of northern India, notably, Bharatpur, Jaipur and Gwalior. Savai Raja Jai Singh, the Governor of Agra, operated from one of these buildings known as Jai Singh Ghera.

The ghat owes its name to the demon Kesi (meaning horse). The powerful demon apparently was instructed by Kans to kill Krishna who

80. Vastra Haran. Datia, circa AD 1780. Courtesy: National Museum, New Delhi.

81. Cheerghat, Vrindavan: the place on the Yamuna bank where Krishna is said to have taken away the clothes of gopis who had disrobed themselves to have a dip in the Yamuna.

was mostly seen along the banks of the Yamuna in the company of gops. The demon in the shape of a horse charged at Krishna with the fury of a hurricane. Krishna remained cool-headed, avoided the charging Kesi and managed to thrust his hand into Kesi's mouth.[66] The demon felt an intense pain in the mouth, lost all his teeth, and ultimately died of suffocation, and fell down. The place, thereby, became famous as Kesighat.

Cheerghat: So named as Krishna collected the clothes of the young gopis bathing in the Yamuna and climbed onto a Kadamb tree nearby leaving them irate. The ladies after finishing the bath found their clothes hanging on the branches of the tree. They implored Krishna to let them have their clothes and thus save them from a sense of shame. Krishna joked with them but ultimately returned the clothes making them realise the danger of entering the river without clothes.[67]

Women continue the practice of tying a piece of cloth on the Kadamb tree growing at the spot where the episode is stated to have occurred. It is believed that any wish made to Krishna when tying the cloth would be fulfilled.

Kalidah:[68] The spot is a reminder of the episode of a fight between Krishna and Kalia, a highly poisonous serpent that had a hideout in the Yamuna. The virulent poison from the snake killed many people as well as the cows that entered the Yamuna either to take a bath or a drink.

Krishna while playing with a ball threw it into the river and then used this as an excuse for jumping from a Kadamb tree into the den of Kalia. After a great struggle, he was able to tame the many-headed serpent and emerged victorious, dancing on the hood of the serpent.

The story has wide acceptance and is well illustrated in paintings, wall hangings and in bronze carvings. The Kadamb tree at the spot is stated to be there from the time of Krishna.

Rangji Ka Mandir:[69] The only temple of its kind in northern India, it combines the traditional style of Gopuram seen in the southern Indian temples of Madurai or Tanjavur and the temple architecture of north India as seen on the main doorway.

82 Deity. Radhavallabh Temple. For about fifty years the deity was in Sevakunj before being moved to the red sandstone temple and finally to the present site.

The inspiration for the temple came from a famous devotee from the south, Shri Rangdeshik. He came north to visit places in Braj and stayed at Govardhan where he was inducted into Vaishnavism by Shrinivasacharya, follower of Shri Ramanuj. The funds for the temple

चवुतरे पर वैठना

84

were provided by a prominent businessman of Mathura who finally became a disciple of Shri Rangdeshik. The temple took ten years to build and was completed in 1902. The principal idol in the temple is of Shri Goda Rangmannar. His wife is Shri Godadevi, also addressed as 'Andala' in the south. Both the names are another version of Krishna and Radha of Braj. Also installed in the temple are idols of Narsingh, Venugopal, Ram, Sita and Lakshman, Sheshashaivishnu, Alwars and Acharya Ramanuj.

83. Imlitala. The place where Shri Chaitanya rested on his first visit to the land of Braj.

84. Raman Reti — drawing the house on sand for Krishna to step in at night.

The main entry to the temple is by the western gate designed in the Rajputana style. It has fine stonework done by artisans from Jaipur. Immediately thereafter is the entrance to the 105 feet high, seven storeyed Gopuram etched with figures of gods and goddesses carved on each storey.

85. Idol of Krishna Kali, Vrindavan.

86. Nimbark Kot Temple, Vrindavan. The main temple is devoted to Nimbark Sampradaya.

86

An interesting object in the inner courtyard is the gold-plated pillar, which is 24 feet deep inside the earth. Some of the festivals, like the temple cart festival, are peculiar to this temple and well-attended by devotees from all parts of India.

Vrindavan has a number of ponds (kunds), but two are outstanding for their mention in mythology, though now they are in a state of disrepair.

Brahmakund:[70] It is located on the north-eastern end of the temple of Rangji. It was near this kund that Brahma realised the strength and divinity of Krishna as the Supreme God and so requested to be pardoned. In later years the kund was again to make history when Mirabai visited Vrindavan and sat on the steps of the kund in song and meditation. The temple of Mirabai with some of the original artefacts and idols is nearby.

Davanalkund:[71] Once there was a widespread forest fire which threatened the life of the cows and calves that were grazing in the pastures. Krishna absorbed the fire in his body, and later cooled himself by bathing at this pond, called Davanalkund since then.

Van (Forests): Vrindavan, as the name suggests, was a *van* (forest). Mostly there were *Tulsi* groves and hence the name Vrinda which is also another name for Tulsi. Even now, practically in each house and temple, Tulsi is venerated, as mythologically Tulsi is also a consort of Krishna. Still there is many a van, though in diminutive size associated with Krishna. A mention has been made earlier of Nidhivan, the meditation abode of Swami Haridas. Others of importance are Sevakunj and Vanshivat.

Sevakunj:[72] It is located adjacent to Nidhivan. The place gained importance during the time of Shri Hitharivansh whose claim to be a disciple of Shri Radha was universally accepted. It is said that he often had visions of both Radha and Krishna. Shri Hitharivansh had apparently been asked by the divine couple not to allow anyone to stay at Sevakunj at night so as not to disturb the privacy of the divine pair.

The garden is full of thick bushes of *Pilu* trees. The divine couple along with their playmates performed *ras* and then rested. Once apparently Shri Lalita had felt thirsty and found no water inside the kunj. Shri Krishna pressed his flute into the ground to create a pond, known subsequently as Lalitakund, which still exists in the kunj.

It is locally claimed that people who had attempted to stay in the Sevakunj or tried to peep from the neighbouring houses have either met tragic death or lost their mental balance. No one stays at Sevakunj after the evening *arti*.

Vanshivat: The call of Krishna's flute from this place used to lead the gops and gopis to assemble for *ras*. The place was once full of Kadamb trees with plenty of birds and animals. Urbanisation has taken a toll resulting in the loss of fauna and flora. However, the magic of Krishna's flute is still remembered and he is venerated at the spot, where he used to stand and play on his magic flute.

Radhadamodar Temple:[73] It was established by Srila Jeev Goswami, nephew of Roop and Sanatan Goswami. Damodar is another name of Krishna. The name of the temple is associated with the episode when Yashoda desired to check the naughty child Krishna and tied him with a rope around his abdomen (*udara*).

During the disturbed period the temple idols were removed to Jaipur. They have been replaced by the replicas of the originals. The temple became the focus of international acclaim because Srila Prabhupad had stayed in this temple for six years before migrating to the USA to spread the message of Krishna's consciousness. The temple is a major attraction for devotees from abroad. Many of them even go through the traditional form of Hindu marriage within the precincts of the temple. One of the unusual articles in the temple is a stone with markings of the feet of Krishna, his staff and flute and his calf. Krishna apparently had given this piece of stone to Shri Sanatan Goswami, asking him to go round the stone piece prior to the morning ritual, as in his old age he would be unable to perform parikrama of Shri Giriraj. The stone piece is not open for public viewing but can be seen for a token offering of a couple of rupees. In the temple courtyard are the samadhis of Shri Roop Goswami and others.

Imlitala: *Imli* (tamarind) is a large tree. This is the tree under which Shri Chaitanya Mahaprabhu had apparently rested during his visit to Vrindavan and had participated in group devotional singing.[74]

Shri Chaitanya Mahaprabhu on his visit to Braj stayed at Akrurghat. He was deeply moved by the spiritual environment of Braj and felt disturbed that Vrindavan, the abode of the divine couple, had turned into a deserted jungle. On his return to Neelanchal he solicited the help of two of his disciples, Roop and Sanatan Goswami, to go to Braj and revive its glory.

87. Offering to Kadamb tree which is associated with the Krishna legend.

Braj Parikrama

89. Govardhan Dharan. Jaipur, early 19th century. Courtesy: National Museum, New Delhi.

Parikrama literally means going around a temple or a place of worship. But in Braj, which is full of temples and places of worship, *parikrama* means going round any one place such as Mathura, Govardhan or Vrindavan or a general tour of the significant places all over Braj. Apparently the first pilgrimage of the holy spots was performed by Udhav, about five thousand years ago, after Krishna had moved to Dwarka. Udhav had requested Krishna to be allowed to stay on at Braj. During his stay he visited all the famous places associated with the life and legend of Krishna.

Bajranabh, the great-grandson of Krishna, had come to know of these places from Udhav and later on, he is reputed to have visited several of them as can be made out from the temples and the idols that were installed by him and which are spread all over Braj.[75] These descriptions are available in the various Puranas. Subsequently, these places remained eclipsed during the Buddhist and Jain period, when the Buddhist monasteries and stupas must have been the main attraction. The description given by the two Chinese travellers Fa-Hien and Hiuen Tsang seems to confirm Mathura's importance as an important place of Buddhist culture.

The legend of Krishna of Braj was revived with the arrival of Shri Nimbarkacharya in the fifteenth century.[76] He stayed at Govardhan and spread the message of Krishna. Shri Narayan Bhatt in his treatise, *Brajbhakti Vilas*, also provided a very detailed description of the sacred places in Braj. He wrote this manuscript in the year 1552 A.D. at Radhakund at the age of fourteen years. It would therefore be natural to conclude that Shri Narayan Bhatt, who considered himself an Avatar of Narada, must have travelled to all the sacred places documenting their location and importance. In 1490 A.D. Acharya Madhvendra Puri performed Braj Yatra.[77] It was only in the sixteenth century that the saints and the sages converged on Mathura Vrindavan to rediscover Braj of Krishna's times. The task was initiated by Mahaprabhu Vallabhacharya who first travelled to Braj in 1555 A.D., followed by a second visit

88. Dandavati Parikrama. It is usually performed on the 18 km route around Govardhan. (On page 113)

90. Braj Parikrama. Thousands of men, women and children undertake this journey barefoot on certain auspicious days of the year.

91. Doodh Ki Dhar Parikrama, Govardhan. Release of a trickle of milk from the earthen pot is expression of devotion when performing circumambulation of Govardhan.

in 1565 A.D His second visit was mostly confined to twelve *vans* and the tour was completed in seven days.[78] Shri Chaitanya Mahaprabhu came to Braj in 1573 A.D. and identified some of the important places associated with Krishna leela.[79] He was deeply moved by seeing the desolate wild countryside, with the temples of faith destroyed or looted of their belongings. He did not stay too long but later on sent his two trusted disciples, Roop and Sanatan Goswami, for the revival of Braj.

In due course was formulated a procedure for undertaking a Braj Yatra. These procedures were laid down by some of the religious scholars of the period, such as Shri Narayan Bhatt, Shri Vitthalnath and others. Shri Vallabhacharya also authored a procedure for the Braj Yatra, commencing at Mathura in which the travellers took the vow of celibacy and observed several rules during their travels, which continue to be followed even today in the Yatras arranged by heads of various religious institutions.

The Yatras were stopped by Aurangzeb, and Braj was once again in turmoil because of the policies followed by the Mughal court. The Yatras were revived once again towards the end of the Mughal rule, especially when Braj came under the protection of the Rajputs and the Scindias. Goswami Purshottam revived the Braj Yatra in the early nineteenth century and it has continued thereafter. A new procedure was laid down for the total coverage of all the places in fifty days.

The tradition of Yatra as seen today is thus an experience of a devotional tour through the important religious places in Braj.[80] Among the long list of saints and sages who helped to restore the cultural heritage of Braj may be mentioned such celebrated figures as Gautam Buddha, Adi Shankaracharya, Vallabhacharya, Chaitanya, Keshav Kashmiri, Mirabai and Raskhan.

Today the groups performing the Yatra assemble on the banks of the Yamuna. Under the guidance of their Guru the group pays homage to Yamuna and Tulsi, invokes the blessings of their deity and takes a vow of celibacy before starting the parikrama.

During the daytime the group visits the important holy places, learns about their importance as described in the scriptures, and participates in religious discourses and devotional singing.

Parikrama may be performed at any time of the year, but there are also special occasions when thousands of people from Braj and other parts of India make their pilgrimage. The main 'parikramas' start after the rainy season. That is the time when the land of Braj washed by the rains appears green, with tender leaves sprouting on bushes and creepers. The birds too fly back and the peacocks dance with the beautiful spread of their feathers. The time spent by the group in going around the places may vary from sixteen to forty-five days.

Traditionally there are seven different types of parikrama:

i) *Panchtirth Parikrama* or a visit to five places of pilgrimage. Is undertaken in August/September and is completed in five days.

ii) *Ramdal Parikrama* is undertaken immediately after Krishna Janmashtami (August). The followers of Ramanand, Shri Chaitanya and Nimbarkacharya undertake this parikrama which is completed in 15-16 days.

iii) *Bari Parikrama* or the grand tour is usually undertaken by the followers of Vallabhacharya and starts at Mathura and is completed in 40 days.

iv) *Other Parikramas*: These are short parikramas specific to a place and performed at any time. The most frequently performed are the parikramas of Mathura, Vrindavan and Govardhan. These parikramas are commonly undertaken on the full moon and a day after the new moon every month. On certain special days a combined parikrama of Mathura and Vrindavan is performed. Shri Narayan Bhatt in his description of the Braj parikramas specified the distances, the places to be visited and the time to be spent on each parikrama.

v) *Dandwati Parikrama*:. Normally all the parikramas are covered on foot. Most of the devotees walk barefooted. But in Dandwati Parikrama, the person literally traverses the distance crawling on his belly. This parikrama can be performed anywhere but the place of choice through the ages has been Govardhan. Some of the devotees decide to perform 108 rounds of Govardhan. This usually takes 2-3 years to complete. Dandwati Parikrama is also performed in Vrindavan.

vi) *Antargrahi Parikrama*: It is mainly confined to the famous religious places in and around Mathura and is usually performed in the month of August. The participants visit Vishram Ghat and the nearby places of importance. This is mostly undertaken by those persons who later have a desire to undertake a Braj parikrama to see other places of importance.

vii) *Mathura Parikrama*: Also described as 5 kos (16 km) parikrama as Mathura is supposed to extend up to 5 kos. Usually this is performed four times in a year.

The Braj parikrama has been covered in some detail in the section on festivals. Although it is not a festival as such, the joyous mood of the participants of a parikrama conveys an air of festivity which is a delight for the photographer.

92. Chakreshwar Mandir. The five-faced Shiva is considered one of the most sacred spots near Mansiganga.

Fairs and Festivals

Jhoola Mahotsav (Swing Festival):[81] Shravan, in the Indian Calendar, corresponding to the months of July and August, revives the parched land with rain after the long spell of summer. The lush green landscape serves as the perfect backdrop for this festival, when the Braj belles in their fineries sway in rope-swings suspended from the branches of mango or neem trees. Their songs, specially composed for the rainy season, are full of episodes describing the meetings of the divine lovers. The festival is celebrated with great splendour at Dwarkadheesh in Mathura, Bihariji and Radharaman temples in Vrindavan, and Shriji's temple at Barsana, where gold and silver swings are brought out to enthrone the deity. Thousands of devotees participate in the festival by visiting these temples every day for almost one month.

For Krishna in Braj, every day had been a day of festivity and excitement shared with playmates and most of all with the divine consort, Shri Radha. That air of festivity never died down even after Krishna's departure from Mathura for Dwarka. Krishna and Radha have continued to inspire the people in Braj who celebrate a large number of Radha-Krishna festivals almost throughout the year. These festivals have a local flavour because of their association with the divine couple. We would start with the festival celebrating the birth of Shri Krishna, popularly known as Janmashtami or Krishna Janmashtami.

Krishna Janmashtami:[82] Krishna was born to Devaki well past midnight on the eighth day of the sixth month of the Indian Calendar. The day is celebrated by the followers of Krishna in Braj for two reasons. One, it marked the beginning of efforts to destroy evil and restore a just socio-religious order. And two, it was an occasion for rejoicing in the house of Nand as, after a long wait, Nand and Yashoda had a male child of a radiant face and bewitching smile. The celebrations in the temples of Braj involve a very elaborate *puja* in the morning commonly described as *Mahabhishek*. This includes the bathing of the idol with Yamuna water brought in silver utensils. The idols are usually brought out of the sacrarium to facilitate public

93. Holi at Phalen. A priest is jumping out of the ritual fire. (On page 123)

94. Lath Ka Mela at Rangji Temple, Vrindavan. People try to climb the wooden pole but are foiled in their attempt by the constant stream of oily water.

95. Shri Krishna Janmashtami. Illuminations at Janmabhoomi Complex, Mathura, on Shri Krishna's birthday.

viewing for the Mahabhishek. A special midnight celebration is held coinciding with the time of the birth of Krishna. The Janmashtami is the time for a large influx of visitors into Mathura from all over India and elsewhere.

Throughout Braj, *ras* is enacted by various professional groups depicting the Krishna leela. These are very popular with the locals as well as visitors from outside.

Lath Ka Mela or Nand Utsav:[83] This festival is peculiar to the Rangji temple. A thirty feet high wooden post is erected near the front gate of Rangji temple. The wooden post is well lubricated with mustard oil which is periodically poured down the post from an elevated *machan* to make it slippery. Young boys try to climb up the post to reach the top and win the competition.

Radha Ashtami:[84] The birthday of Shri Radha is celebrated 15 days after Krishna Janmashtami. Whereas Krishna's birth is marked with solemnity, Radha's birth celebrations are marked with joy and abandon. The centre of festivities remains Barsana, the land of Shri Radha, specially her temple on top of the Brahma hill.

Visitors and devotees go round Barsana in groups singing devotional songs in praise of Shri Radha. The Goswamis from Nandgaon join their counterpart at Shriji temple at Barsana for joint singing of devotional songs invoking the blessings of Shri Radha.

Celebrations are also held in places and temples associated with her memory, for example, the temple of Radhavallabh at Vrindavan as also at Sevakunj. In the Radhavallabh temple, the celebrations start with the distribution of clothes, cereals, fruits and sweets to all and sundry. The climax is reached by pouring yellow-coloured milk over the devotees. The colour is associated with the excrement of a new-born infant. The singing and dancing, and spells of the spray of saffron-coloured milk keep the devotees amused and provide a lot of excitement to the spectators in the galleries above. The groups then move to Sevakunj, the garden associated with the visitations of the divinity every night.

Vijayadashmi: In the month of October, the important festival of Vijayadashmi, also known as Dussehra, is celebrated. It commemorates the victory of Ram over Ravan.[85] Giant cardboard effigies of the ten-headed Ravan are placed at public places and at the end of the day set on fire (to simulate cremation), marking the death of Ravan and symbolically the victory of righteousness over evil. This festival is celebrated over a large part of India. But for Mathura, it has a special

96

97

96. Shri Krishna's birthday celebrations at Radharaman Temple, Vrindavan.

97. Shri Krishna's birthday celebrations at Bhagavat Bhawan Temple, Mathura.

98. Radha Ashtami at Barsana

98

appeal, as the city, a legend has it, was founded by Shatrughan, the youngest brother of Shri Ram.

The fifteen-day period preceding Dussehra is known as Pitra Paksh. During this period, the Sanjhi motifs are painted on the walls of individual homes, or arranged with dry colours in the temples. The folk art of the individual houses and the more sophisticated art form of the temples will be discussed in the section on the creative and performing arts of Braj.

100

Sharad: The full-moon night in October after the rainy season is very special for the people in Braj. On this night Krishna performed the *maharas* with the gopis.[86] The festivities during the day recall the Krishna leela and at night there is the enactment of the *maharas.* The deity is specially dressed in silver attire for the occasion.

Deepavali and Deepdan:[87] Deepavali, the festival of lights, is one of the most important festivals celebrated throughout India. The festival gathers an added momentum in Braj because of its association with an episode in the life of Krishna. According to the Krishna legend, the gops and gopis of Braj came to light the lamps on Govardhan hill as a mark of their devotion and respect for their saviour Krishna, as Giriraj. On Deepavali night the Giriraj — Govardhan — is lit by thousands of lamps. The maximum concentration is on the steps of Mansiganga near the temple of Giriraj.

99. Samaj—group singing at Shriji Temple, Barsana, on the occasion of Radha Ashtami.

100. Maharas at Sharad Utsav, Vrindavan. Autumn is the season for the dance dramas relating to Radha and Krishna.

101

Govardhanpuja is celebrated on the day after Deepavali. On this day the people invoke the blessings of Giriraj who had, according to legend, protected them from a deluge caused by incessant rains. The puja is carried out on the Govardhan hills, in the temples or even in the homes. Those living away from the hills usually make a model of Govardhan out of cowdung. In the temples the puja is offered in an elaborate style.

In the area around Govardhan, the celebrations begin with the offering of milk to the deity, who is venerated as another form of Krishna. Thousands of litres of milk is poured on the stone face in various temples. There is a continuous stream of visitors, mostly barefoot, to famous temples like Danghati, Mansiganga and Jatipura.

In the evening, all stone faces are washed for the special make-up and display of Giriraj in the form that the people have known and worshipped. The most important and attractive form is at Jatipura which is also the place where the idol of Shri Nathji is supposed to have revealed itself. The evening *shringar* (make-up) of the rock face is in the form of Shri Nathji of Nathdwara.

101. Deepdan at Mansiganga, Govardhan. Oil lamps are offered at Mansiganga on the night of Diwali.

102. Illuminations at Mansiganga, Govardhan.

Yamdwitiya. This festival falls in the month of Kartik (October-November) on the third day after Deepavali. On this day brothers and sisters take dips in the river Yamuna.[88] The bathing ghats in Braj and specially Vishramghat attract thousands of devotees on the occasion. Yam, the god of death, is supposedly the brother of Yamuna and offerings are made on this day by sisters for the general protection and well-being of their brothers. In the rest of India this festival is known as Bhai Duj.

Basant Panchami: The end of February almost marks the end of the winter season. The mustard crop is in full bloom and the landscape of Braj turns into a sea of tiny pale yellow flowers. This heralds the coming of the spring season which is celebrated as a festival called 'Basant Panchami' (spring).[89] Pale yellow is the colour that predominates in all the festivities ranging from the dresses worn by local devotees, the idol's decorations, and the festive flower arrangements made. One of the most interesting decorations is in the temple of Shahji where the 'basantikamra' (Yellow Room), with a completely yellow decor, is opened only once a year on this day for the enthronement of the idol.

103. Festival of lights, Govardhan.

Holi: Holi or the festival of colours is celebrated about ten days after the spring festival. A delightful visual, this festival combines the gaiety of a carnival and the devotional flavour of a religious festival with the singing of amorous songs as unbridled expressions of youth. This is the time when both feelings and colours run riot. Braj seems to be the only place where one comes across a variety of forms in which the festival of Holi is celebrated. The following account records in brief some of the most colourful and ecstatic forms of Holi in Braj.

Holi at Phalen:[90] The festival starts with the burning of a huge pyre of wood on the night of the full moon in the month of March. This practice is associated with a mythological story according to which the tyrant king (Hirnakashyap), who could not accept his son Prahlad turning to God and faith, ordered his sister Holika to sit on a burning pyre so as to burn Prahlad alive. Although Holika had been blessed with the power that the fire would not burn her, she did get burnt to death and Prahlad instead came out unscathed. Since then, the burning of a pyre of wood on this day symbolises the victory of good over evil.

The Holi at Phalen village re-enacts the Prahlad-Holika episode. The ritual of the lighting of the pyre of wood acquires a dramatic turn when one of the local priests walks through the fire unscathed.

Holi at Barsana:[91] The seat of Shri Radha has all the touch of romanticism. The songs sung by people recall the pranks of Radha and Krishna and their love for each other and the gopis. The visitors move around in large and small groups singing, dancing and applying colours, intoxicated with the thoughts of Radha and Krishna leela. The climax of the festivities is in the afternoon when the gops of Nandgaon come to Barsana to play Holi with the local gopis. The women play Holi by hitting the men hard with a 2-1/2 metre long bamboo staff. The men (gops) protect themselves with shields. The violence of the attack is mellowed down by the singing of folk songs specially composed for the occasion which express, in a variety of ways, how the Holi festival had enraptured the belles of Barsana.

Holi at Nandgaon:[92] The following day the entire scene is re-enacted at Nandgaon. The gops of Barsana are invited to play Holi with the village belles of Nandgaon. The elaborate procedure includes carrying the flag of the temple of Shriji. The flag is received by the gops of Barsana with devotional singing, and is carried on foot to Nandgaon where all attempts to capture it are foiled by the visiting group.

The rest of the festivities at Nandgaon mark devotional singing in the temple, folk singing on the streets followed by the women emerging in a group to play Holi with bamboo staffs.

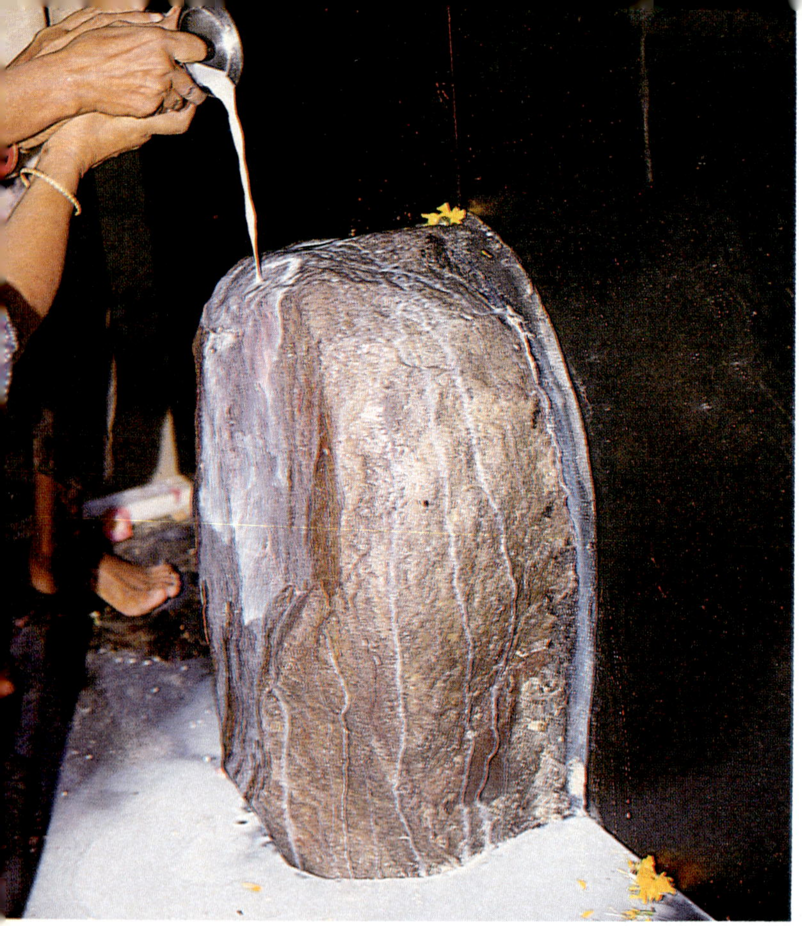

104

105

106

107

104. Offering of milk to Shri Giriraj Govardhan, Jatipura.

105. Shri Nathji shringar resembles very closely the shringar of Shri Nathji at Nathdwara near Udaipur in Rajasthan.

106. Chhappan (56) Bhog Giriraj Govardhan. The figure fifty-six refers to the variety of food offerings made to the deity on festive days.

107. Prakatya of Shri Nathji — Giriraj Govardhan. Private collection.

108

109

108. Shops at Vrindavan during festival time.

109 Govardhan Puja at Govindji Temple, Vrindavan.

110. Holi: the festival of colours.

111

Holi at Dauji:[93] It stands out for the wild abandon with which it is celebrated. The women assemble with buckets of coloured water which are poured on the menfolk who are also thrashed with whips made out of cloth torn from men's dresses. The rules of the game do not permit the menfolk to touch the bodies of the women or unveil their faces. The emptying of basketful of colour powder from the roof of the temple creates a thick haze of different hues which spares none, neither participants nor onlookers!

111. Holi revelry.

112. Krishna playing Holi. Private collection.

113

113. Flag of Shriji Temple, Barsana.

114. Holi, Barsana festival.

Brahmutsav:[94] Popularly known as Rath ka Mela at Rangji temple, this festival marks the end of the fifteen-day festivities of Holi starting at Barsana. In this festival, the deity is taken out on a fifteen-metre high chariot, pulled by devotees, from the main temple to the gardens of Rangji and back.

Akshaytritiya:[95] This is the only occasion in a year when the idols are venerated in a simple form divested of the usual adornments and fineries. The idol of Bankebihari is visited by a large number of

114

devotees anxious to see the feet of the idol simply adorned with anklets. In other temples, the idols are decorated with sandalwood paste. Some of the notable ones are Garudgovind where one can see the twelve-handed idol of Govindji mounted on the celestial bird Garud, Govinddev where Shriji is seen holding a calf, and Radha Raman where one is struck by the small size of the idol as it emerged from a Saligram.

115. Lath mar Holi at Barsana. It is celebrated a week in advance of the celebrations elsewhere. The main action centres around women who sing taunting songs and finally hit men with large bamboo sticks.

116. Huranga at Dauji Temple: wild display of Holi fun and frolics.

116

अलबेले
श्री दाऊजी की

दमा दमन
पंखा

117. Huranga at Dauji Temple: wild display of Holi fun and frolics.

118. Rath Ka Mela at Rangji Temple marks the end of the month-long Holi festivities.

119. House of Nandbaba, Mahavan.

120. Jehar Puja singing and dancing to make offerings to Lord Shiva for the birth of a male child.

121. Kanwar carriers carry holy water from the Ganges to the Shiva temple.

Devotees

123. Samadhi of Sanatan Goswami, Vrindavan. The learned disciple of Shri Chaitanya helped rediscover Braj.

The devotees of Krishna, through the years, have helped recreate the places associated with Krishna leela in Braj and spread the theme of Krishnaism i.e. the concept of Krishna as Vishnu incarnate. Braj with its nucleus at Mathura had gone through a number of cycles of plunder and devastation followed by reconstruction. The hordes of the Ghaznavis, Khiljis and Lodis had plundered and destroyed the physical, fiscal, social and cultural heritage of Braj, which had accumulated over many centuries. Mathura had been reduced to a ramshackle small town and Vrindavan, true to its name, had become one vast jungle as sighted by Chaitanya Mahaprabhu from Akrurghat.[96]

How could the places be rediscovered and even rehabilitated? It was entirely because the image of Krishna and the concept of Krishna leela had been kept alive throughout India. The land associated with Krishna kept attracting people with faith in Krishnaism to visit Braj and revive its lost splendour. Let us briefly scan the period from the time of Bajranabh.

Bajranabh, the great-grandson of Shri Krishna, with the help of Sandilya Rishi, undertook the work of rediscovering Braj. The first graphic account of the places in Braj associated with Krishna leela emerged from there.[97] But it was left to the devotees of Krishna who came from different parts of India and converged on Braj to rediscover and revitalise these places, on which the forces of destruction through the long years had taken a heavy toll. They stayed to write scriptures, compose poems, and develop styles of creative and performing arts with Krishna as the central theme. Thus Vaishnavism, as Krishnaism, revived itself in Braj and spread far and wide. This section will devote itself to a brief description of the contribution of the devotees who spread the message of Krishna.

122. Shri Chaitanya Mahaprabhu, a fervent devotee of Shri Krishna, who visited Braj in the early sixteenth century and initiated efforts for the revival of Braj. (On page 151)

These devotees came to Mathura and Vrindavan from all over India because they had a dream, an inner call or a strong desire to see for themselves the land of their deity — Krishna. With their cumulative

124. Sanatan Goswami's place of meditation at Vrindavan.

efforts they achieved a renaissance in the cultural and spiritual heritage of Braj and re-established Vaishnavism with Krishṇa as the Supreme Godhead. This process spans a period of over two hundred and fifty to three hundred years, starting with Nimbarkacharya as founder of one of the four Vaishnav *sampradayas*.

Despite subtle distinctions, all followers of various *sampradayas* (groups) agree on Shrimad Bhagvat as the fountain-head of their religious thoughts and Krishna of Braj as the mortal form of Narayan or Vishnu. A scholarly work studying in depth the writings and life-style of the saints of Mathura and Vrindavan is *Bhaktmal* or stories of the saints, compiled during the reign of Akbar by Nabhaji. In the very first couplet he writes, '*Bhakta bhakti bhagvant guru, chatur nam vapu ek*' or Devotee, Devotion, God and Guru (Teacher) all imply only one thing i.e. God.[98]

Nimbarkacharya:[99] The oldest sect in Vaishnavism is Nimbark or Sankadiksampradaya whose founder was Shri Bhaskaracharya. The word Nimbar literally means 'sun over a neem' (Margosa) tree. This unusual prefix to the title of a sampradaya is associated with an unusual incident which supposedly happened during the time of Nimbarkacharya. Once Bhaskaracharya had invited an ascetic (Bairagi) to dine with him during the daytime, since according to his religious code, the Bairagi did not partake of food after sunset. It so happened, however, that the swami and the ascetic engrossed in discussions forgot about the time. When they finally emerged from their room, the last rays of the setting sun were just filtering through the neem tree. Bhaskaracharya requested the Sungod to let the rays of the sun linger on the neem tree until the guest had been fed. This wish was granted. Henceforth Bhaskaracharya was called Nimbark or Nimbaditya. There are different versions about the period of Nimbark (from Dwaparyug to 13th century). He is stated to have settled first at Dhruvteela near Mathura and then moved to Neemgaon near Govardhan. Later Keshav Dev Bhatt, the thirty-third acharya of the sampradaya, added to the theological basis of the sampradaya, by emphasising the precedence of devotional to academic or intellectual practices.

Gaudiasampradaya:[100] The Gaudiasampradaya includes Shri Chaitanya Mahaprabhu, its founder, and his devoted disciples, namely Roop and Sanatan Goswami, Jeev Goswami, Raghunath Bhatt Goswami, Gopal Bhatt Goswami, Raghunathdas Goswami and Krishna Das Kaviraj.

Chaitanya Mahaprabhu, the founder of Gaudiasampradaya, was the first to make efforts for the revival of places related to Krishna which had almost disappeared. Shri Chaitanya's two major contributions are inaugurating the Sankirtan movement and initiating work on the revival of places associated with Krishna leela.

Chaitanya Mahaprabhu visited Mathura and Vrindavan when he was twenty-nine years old and stayed for about a year. On coming to Mathura, he is believed to have had a dip at Vishramghat and proceeded to all the holy places in and around Mathura, Vrindavan. When he visited the two lakes described as Gauri and Kali, he was able to identify them as Radhakund and Shyamkund and stated that these two lakes are the holiest places in the universe. While at Vrindavan he rested under the tamarind tree which even then had a

125

reputation of being as old as the Dwaparyug. Chaitanya Mahaprabhu believed that Krishna is Vishnu incarnate. His sermons emphasised five codes of conduct: (1) keep company with the devotees of Krishna, (2) chant and hear the word Krishna all the time, (3) participate in discourses to hear the name of Krishna, (4) visit Vrindavan, and (5) worship the image of Krishna individually or perform Kirtan. His concept of devotional group singing ran across all caste barriers and opened the door of bhakti to those who would not be allowed to enter the temples. This was a silent reform that crept into the religious ceremonies and before long Krishna Sankirtan became the most popular form of devotional singing.

126

127

125. Shri Vallabhacharya, Pushtimargi, founder of Vallabh Sampradaya.

126. Surdas — a painting from private collection.

127. Samadhi of Surdas.

128 129

On his return from Braj, Chaitanya Mahaprabhu ordained the brothers Roop and Sanatan Goswami, who were his prominent disciples, to go to Braj and help in the rediscovery of the important places.[101] They were also given the task to document and systematise Gaudia Vaishnav philosophy as expounded by Mahaprabhu himself. Some of the important books written by Roop Goswami include *Bhaktirasamrit Sindhu*, which details the steps of becoming one with the godhead; *Widagdhamadhav*, a drama based on Krishna leela in Vrindavan; and *Ujwalnilmani*, an account of transcendental love for the godhead. A prolific writer, some of his other writings include *Mathura Mahatmya, Updeshamrit, Lalit Madhav, Padyavali, Hansdoot, Udhavsandesh, Dankelikaumudi.*

According to a popular story, Roop Goswami once had a dream, in which a dark complexioned boy informed him that he was lying buried on Goma Teela (mound). The next day with the help of some people, Roop Goswami dug up the area and uncovered the idol of Govinddev which had been crafted during the time of Bajranabh.[102]

130

131

128. Swami Hari Das, the saint whose devotional music reached sublime heights. A painting from personal collection.

129. Belongings of Swami Hari Das, Nidhi Van, Vrindavan.

130. Nidhi Van, Vrindavan, where Mughal Emperor Akbar, accompanied by Tansen, met Swami Hari Das.

131. Samadhi of Swami Hari Das, Nidhi Van.

132. Shri Hitharivanshji, founder of Radha Vallabh Sampradaya, who built the Radha Vallabh Temple, Vrindavan.

The idol was installed at the mound where it was revealed. Later on, the idol of Radha Rani was brought from Radhanagar, Orissa, to be installed in the same temple. Apparently this deity was also revealed in the course of another dream sequence seen by Raja Purshottam of Orissa. In years to come, the idol of Govinddev was enshrined in one of the most beautiful temples in north India.

Roop Goswami continued his spiritual and literary activities almost to the end. He withdrew from active life on hearing of the death of Chaitanya Mahaprabhu and also Sanatan Goswami. Finally he handed over charge of religious matters to Jeev Goswami and left the mortal world in 1621 A.D. His samadhi is in the eastern part of Radha Damodar temple.[103]

Sanatan Goswami, brother of Roop Goswami, also came to Braj as instructed by Chaitanya Mahaprabhu. He had been working as a minister in the court of Hussainshah of Gaur (Bengal) and gave up the life of royal comforts to become the disciple of Shri Chaitanya. Arriving in Braj, he lived in many places such as Gokul, Mahavan, Nandgaon, Radhakund and the longest in Vrindavan. He initiated the procedure for the *seva* (service) of Madan Mohan (Krishna). Later on a businessman, Ramdas Kapur, helped to construct the red sandstone temple on Dwadashaditya Teela.

Sanatan Goswami's daily routine apparently included a parikrama on foot of the Govardhan, the total distance from Vrindavan to Govardhan and back being approximately 54 km. When he grew old, it was rumoured that Madan Mohan appeared before him in person and offered him a piece of stone with footprints of Shri Krishna. Sanatan Goswami was advised to do parikrama around the stone which would earn him the merit of going around Govardhan. This stone piece is still preserved in the Radha Damodar temple.

The important writings of Sanatan Goswami include *Haribhaktvilas, Vrahadbhagwatamrit* and others.

Jeev Goswami: Jeev Goswami was a devoted nephew of Roop and Sanatan Goswami who had migrated from Bengal to make a deep study of the writings of Roop and Sanatan Goswami. His main contribution lay in the development of the literature on Braj and the devotional aspects of Vaishnav thought. He was the first in Vrindavan to use paper for writing a manuscript, which was hitherto written on tree bark (bhojpatra). His important writings include *Shatsandarbh, Kram Sandarbh, Durgam Sangamani, Ramlochan Rochni, Gopal Champu,* etc. He is also remembered for having developed a treatise on grammar titled

Harinamvrat. In 1599 A.D. he catalogued the Seva style for Radha Damodar in the form in which he had worshipped the Lord.

He died in 1660 A.D. His meditation hut and samadhi are both located within the precincts of Radha Damodar temple.[104]

Raghunath Bhatt Goswami: He was an important disciple of Chaitanya Mahaprabhu. He was born and brought up at Kashi where he learnt the scriptures and was specially impressed by the religious discourses of Shri Chaitanya. After the death of his parents, encouraged by Mahaprabhu, he moved to Vrindavan. At this time Roop Goswami was still alive and Raghunath Bhatt was given the task of popularising Krishnabhakti among the lay public. He undertook this task by organising discourses on Shrimad Bhagwat at Govindji temple. He was famous for his orations and his rendering of devotional songs. His fame for holding religious discourses spread far and wide and even Raja Mansingh of Jaipur came under his spell. The present-day Govinddev temple was erected by Raja Mansingh as an expression of his devotion to Raghunath Bhatt.

Raghunath Bhatt apparently did not write but condensed and recited the scriptures in the language that the people could easily understand. He took as his disciple Swami Gadadhar Bhatt who came from South India, and died in 1620 A.D. His samadhi is located near Rangji temple at Vrindavan.

Gopal Bhatt Goswami: Born in 1557 A.D. on the banks of the river Kaveri, Gopal Bhatt Goswami came under the influence of Shri Chaitanya during the latter's tour of South India. Consequently, he renounced the material world, and came to Govardhan in order to meditate and attend religious discourses. He joined Roop Goswami in reviving the places associated with Krishna. Chaitanya Mahaprabhu, on hearing about the arrival of Gopal Bhatt in Braj, apparently sent his personal belongings for him as a present. These included the Tulsi rosary, his apparel and the mat used for meditation and prayers. All these objects are still preserved in Vrindavan.

However, the most interesting story relates to his personal interaction with the Lord. It is said that he had a dark-coloured stone (Saligram) which he worshipped every day. He often thought how much nicer it would have been if this Saligram were an idol of Krishna. The Lord apparently granted his wish and the stone was turned into the idol of Shri Krishna. It was named Radha Raman and installed in the Radha Raman temple in 1599 A.D. where it exists even today. Gopal Bhatt Goswami wrote some books, the famous one being *Hari Bhakti Vilas.*

Raghunath Das Goswami: A disciple of Chaitanya Mahaprabhu, Raghunath Das Goswami had been presented with a Tulsi rosary and black stone (Saligram) which he venerated throughout his life.[105] He helped in the contributions to *Chaitanya Charitramrit, Stavawali Mukta Charitra, Dankeli Chintamani.* He died at Radhakund where his samadhi still exists.

Vallabhacharya: Born into a Telanga Brahmin family from South India, Vallabhacharya blazed a trail of Vaishnavism throughout India. At the age of eleven years he held public discussions with the court pandits at Vijayanagar and kept them spellbound by his mastery of theology and religion. He was at once recognised as the young leader endowed with ability to serve as a spiritual guide. He visited most of the religious places in India and finally came to Gokul. It is said that Yamuna appeared before him in person and pointed to Gokul and the place where Vasudev had landed at Gokul with the basket containing the infant Krishna. The meditation hut Vallabhacharya built in the later part of the fifteenth century still remains intact. Apparently in answer to his prayers Krishna ordained him to preach a new religion of love, and devotion central to which would be the theme of Krishna as Balgopal. Such a concept was to grow as 'Pushtimarg' with Vallabhacharya as the fountain-head of the religious movement.[106] The followers of this sect by tradition and practice are not austere but live a life of comfort and relative ease.

Vallabhacharya established the temple for Shrinathji in 1559 A.D. at Govardhan. The remnants of the original temple can still be seen as a part of the present-day temple. The deity was removed from Govardhan and is at Nathdwara near Udaipur in Rajasthan. It is considered to be the main temple for the followers of Vallabhacharya. In Braj one can see the meditation huts of Vallabhacharya at various places such as Bhandirvan, Govardhan, Radhakund, Mathura and Vrindavan. They are maintained by the followers of Vallabh Sampradaya.

After the death of Vallabhacharya and his eldest son Gopinath, his second son Vitthalnath was made the head of the sect.[107] His single-minded application and religious zeal to spread the message of Krishna is well documented in a Hindi treatise called *Dosaubavan Vaishnavon Ki Varta* (meaning two hundred and fifty-two Vaishnav stories). Vitthalnath's efforts were mainly directed to western India i.e. Gujarat and Kathiawar. He was a regular visitor to Dwarka and en route would often visit Shrinathji. It is therefore no wonder that people from Gujarat and Kathiawar are ardent worshippers of Shrinathji. Vitthalnath died at the age of seventy at the Govardhan hills. The spot is marked by a small hut at the base of Govardhan hills, near the temple of Shrinathji.

133

134

135

33. Samadhis of the Gaudia devotees, Radhadamodar Temple, Vrindavan.

34. Chausath (64) Mahant Ki Samadhi, Vrindavan.

35. Loknath Goswami Ki Samadhi, Vrindavan. He was the first disciple of Shri Chaitanya to visit Braj.

136. Gopal Bhatt's samadhi near Radharaman Temple, Vrindavan. He is stated to have witnessed the transformation of saligram into human form of Radharamanji.

137. Samadhi of Shyama Nand Mahaprabhu, Vrindavan. He was a devotee of Shri Radha. Forehead sectarian markings of his followers resemble the toe-ring of Shri Radha.

136

137

138

139

Shri Krishnadas: Initiated into the sect by Vallabhacharya, Shri Krishnadas was a contemporary of Surdas and was a reputed composer and singer. He claimed to have been in the presence of Lord Krishna many a time. His end came through an accident in the valley of the Giriraj ranges.

During the period from the mid-fifteenth to the late sixteenth century, many devotees of Shrinathji and the followers of Vitthalnath claimed to have had divine visions of Shri Krishna. Devotees such as Shri Nanddas, Shri Chaturbhujdas, Shri Chheetswami, and Shri Govindswami lived, meditated and finally died around Govardhan or Vrindavan area.

Raskhan: Raskhan was a Pathan (with possible connections with the royal family of Afghanistan) who became an ardent follower of Vitthalnathji. He became a keen devotee of Krishna and became celebrated for the poetry he composed in praise of Krishna. He wrote in the simple local dialect (Braj) eulogising Krishna and creating a picture in words which was vivid, ornamental and sensuous.

Raskhan, prior to his life in Braj, was a worldly man with a zest for life. Vitthalnath channelised his thoughts in a single-minded devotion for Krishna. He is entombed under the red sandstone canopy near Gokul, beside his sister's grave.

Rasikbhakt: Almost all the famous devotees of this group lived during the reign of the great Mughals, Akbar and Jahangir. All of them considered Lord Krishna to be the incarnation of Narayana and spread their spiritual message through the word, music and other performing arts. Harivyasdev made his mark by translating Sanskrit texts into the local dialect. His major work, *Maharani*, is considered to be the most important text of the Nimbarksampradaya. It describes the glory of Radha and Krishna leela, emphasises the importance of Vrindavan, home of the divine lovers and devotees, and documents the important festivals held in Braj associated with the divine couple. This group emphasises both devotional and amorous aspects of love between Radha and Krishna, the beloved and the 'lover' in sensuous and divine contacts. On this theological plane Radha is seen as the source of strength for the power personified as Krishna. If Krishna is the ultimate object of love and devotion, then Radha is the picture incarnate of that love. In this group are included Narayan Bhatt, Harivyas Devacharya, Hitharivansh Goswami, Hariram Vyas and Swami Haridas. The theme of celestial love represented by Radha and Krishna was elaborated and choreographed at a later date, by one of the Nimbark followers as "*Ras Leela*", a form of dance drama.

The Famous Trio (Hari Tri): Swami Haridas, Hitharivansh and Hariram Vyas formed an inspired trio dedicated to the cause of Radha-Krishna

138. The ISKCON devotees at Krishna Balram Temple, Vrindavan.

139. Devotional congregation at Jai Singh Ghera, Vrindavan.

worship. All the three were giants in their creative work which included poetry, music and dance. They claimed to have had divine visions of Radha and Krishna in various forms in which they were worshipped. For example, Hitharivansh worshipped Radha as the divinity that provided love and strength to Krishna himself. He claimed to have been visited by Radha and Krishna who revealed the intricacies of the celestial dance form, the *Ras Leela*. Swami Haridas, the ascetic singer, was the follower of Banke Bihari. His high proficiency in music came to be well known. The great Mughal Emperor Akbar visited Swami Haridas in Vrindavan and showed respect to the guru of his court musician, Tansen, appearing barefoot in his presence. The place where Swami Haridas sang his devotional music and kept his frugal belongings is still preserved in Vrindavan. Hariram Vyas too claimed divine visions of Radha and Krishna whom he regularly worshipped. He was well known for his contribution to devotional music and dance.

Three temples in Vrindavan, namely, Radhavallabh, Banke Bihari and Jugalkishore, established with the help of these devotees and their successors, continue to draw the largest number of visitors throughout the year.

Pandas and Goswamis: No description of the devotees can be complete without mentioning the 'Pandas' and the Goswamis. They are the link between the religious and cultural past and the present-day pilgrims who visit the temples and other places of pilgrimage in Braj. They recount the past, enable a person to solemnize rituals of devotion and seek Krishna's blessings on behalf of the devotees. In brief, any aspect of social, cultural, spiritual and religious activity in Braj would be either guided or spearheaded by the Pandas or Goswamis.

Who are these people by origin who have such a hold on the religious conscience of the people? Traditionally the Pandas claim to have descended from their ancestor 'Krishna Das'. He was the Brahmin who helped Chaitanya Mahaprabhu as a guide during his visit to Braj. Since then this group has continued to serve as guides to religious places, and solemnize rituals either at Yamuna or any other holy place in Braj.

They have in the past maintained the tradition of keeping in touch with visitors and their families whom they helped during their visit to Braj. This tradition is followed even today. They maintain meticulous records of each visit of their guest pilgrims. They talk in more than five to six languages of India besides their own Braj Bhasha which is an offshoot of Hindi language.

The Goswamis venerated both for their intellect and devotion to Krishna also trace their origin to the time of the arrival of Chaitanya

140. Swami Akhanda Nanda, one of the well-known saints of this century. A painting.

Mahaprabhu. A mention has been made of Sanatan and Roop Goswami, the two very learned disciples of Shri Chaitanya who served him in propagating Krishna cult. As such the Goswamis have the major responsibility for conducting daily rituals for their presiding deity. In a way all the famous temples in Braj belong to a group or subgroup of Goswamis.

141. Tying nuptial knots: marriage of devotees at Radhadamodar Temple, Vrindavan.

Creative and Performing Arts

143. Shringar of Balgopal. It is the most popular form for household temples in Braj.

The description of Krishna as Rasshiromani projects a new dimension into his multifaceted personality. He is presented as the celestial dancer from whom came the inspiration for various dance and art forms that grew in the Braj area. The cultural heritage emanating from Krishna was nurtured by the Yadavas and the Nagvanshis. The Yadavas, with whom Krishna spent his childhood, were interested in fine arts. Their dance forms hallisak and dandya[108] were a part of their social life. The Nagvanshis, who lived in Mathura after the Yadavas, were also fond of singing and dancing and hence the interest in the fine arts continued to grow.

The renaissance of Braj culture in the fifteenth and sixteenth centuries A.D. came with the convergence of saints and sages from all over India on Braj. A great incentive was provided for devotional songs, group singing, dance drama and many other music forms. Love and veneration for Krishna in Braj added colour to the development of all art forms. The child Krishna entering into dialogues with Yashoda provided the theme for the songs and the poetry of Surdas and Raskhan. The sensual poetry of Bihari portrayed the interaction between the divine lovers. The music of Swami Haridas rose to celestial heights, depicting in his songs the glory of Radha and Krishna. The contributions of Shri Hitharivansh to the lyrical content and Shri Narayan Bhatt to the dance content of the *ras*, dance drama form, are well known. There is an endless variety of art forms which have come to be associated with Braj. Here the description is restricted to a few of the major forms.

Haveli Style Temples and Wall Paintings: The 'haveli'[109] or house-like architecture of the temples grew out of the necessity of preventing them from being singled out as places of worship. This style of architecture is visible in the temples of Dwarkadheesh, Gokul Nath, Bihariji, Radha Raman, Radha Vallabh and many others. The art work is mainly seen in the form of wall paintings.

142. Intricate geometrical pattern: Sanjhi at Shri Radha Madan Mohanji Temple, Vrindavan. (On page 171)

144. Vasudeva carrying infant Krishna to Gokul. Stone carving, Kushan period. From Mathura Museum.

145. Govardhan Leela, late Gupta period. From Mathura Museum.

144

145

With the exodus of the main deities from the temples of Braj to princely protection in the states of Rajasthan, the icon-makers, artists and craftsmen also shifted to Jaipur and the artists known for wall paintings went to Nathdwara.

During recent years, the interest in wall paintings has been revived with the work carried out at Krishna Janmabhumi complex, at the temple of Shriji at Barsana and several other places.

Sanjhikala:[110] Sanjhi is an art form, which uses dry colour powder to portray the Krishna leela. Flower petals are also used to produce artistic designs. These graphic forms are made usually during the fifteen days preceding Dussehra. They can be drawn on earthen or metal surfaces, and even over and under the surface of water when expertly crafted. The graphics made on the watery surface and then immersed in the Yamuna manage to retain their original form. The Sanjhi festival is associated with the evening and revolves around Shri Radha who supposedly inspired and also initiated this art form.[111]

Sanjhi as a folk art is still practised by girls in the rural parts of Braj and in neighbouring states. The children use clay and cowdung as basic material for the designs. The decorations are made using a variety of materials such as flowers, confetti, different coloured pulses, rice, etc. On the last day a very elaborate Sanjhi described as 'Kot' is made which is immersed in running water the next day.

Phoolbangla:[112] With the onset of summer the sweet fragrance of jasmine fills the air around the main temples in Vrindavan. This is the time when flowers are used to design and decorate a 'phoolbangla' a house of flowers, where the deity is installed in the evening. Elaborate flower decorations are made from April to July. In the temple of Bihariji the floral decor is changed daily. These houses of flower are designed by highly skilled craftsmen who have learnt the art as a family tradition. The framework of the house structure is made of bamboo or wood with a criss-cross pattern of nails jutting out of the frame to hold the flower strings in position.

The elaborateness of the floral display depends on the nature of orders placed by various devotees. However, craftsmen are able to maintain the intricate aesthetic beauty of their creation irrespective of the size of flower house. Jasmine flowers are mostly used for the decor though in some temples roses and marigolds are also used. An important accessory for decoration is the soft inner core of the banana stem which is cut into fancy shapes. Usually a dark blue or black background is used to highlight the artistry of these flower arrangements, with suitable lighting doors, windows and the balcony of flowers providing a spectacular view.

147

Jhanki (tableau): Depicting scenes from the life of Krishna, the *Jhanki* tableaus are mostly seen in the temples on festive occasions like the birthday of Shri Krishna. Some of the new temples like Krishna Baldev have permanent tableau displays in the temple precincts.

Idol-making: The artists of Braj through the ages have designed stone idols and made decorations for Buddhist, Jain and Vaishnavite temples. A visit to the Mathura museum indicates the variety of pink stone artefacts belonging to different periods. The craftsmen were also adept in making silver and gold carriages (vahana) for the deity to be taken out of the temple. They made toys in gold and silver to be used as decoration pieces in the temples. During the medieval period the icon-makers shifted to Jaipur where the deity Govind Devji was taken. Later on, while some returned to Braj the majority stayed back to promote the art of icon-making in marble, a speciality of Jaipur.

At present the craftsmen in Mathura keep busy producing icons of Radha, Krishna, Shri Chaitanya and others in soapstone, marble and brass. The most popular form of Krishna is the 'Ladoo Gopal', the crawling child holding a *ladoo* (a round sweetmeat) in one hand.

Shringar of the Idol: Dressing the deity to suit the different festive occasions has been perfected to an art. In Braj, there are three important aspects of the shringar: one, the popularity of the child form of Krishna (Ladoo Gopal); two, the use of the peacock feather, traditionally associated with the headwear of Krishna, for making a variety of headgears; and, finally, the Radha-Krishna theme which is inspired in various designs of shringar including dress styles, ornaments, the mukut (crown), etc.

146. Krishna Swaroop: a boy dressed as Krishna for the ras.

147. Silver crowns made by local craftsmen. They are usually used for 'Sharad' ras.

148

149

148. Brass idol maker. Vrindavan.

149. Balgopal made of brass.

150. Stone idol makers of Vrindavan.

151. Tulsi Mala — beads made from the stems of tulsi plant.

150

151

152

153

154

Originally gold and silver were used profusely for the decoration of the idols. Precious metals and gems becoming prohibitively expensive, synthetic material is being increasingly used today resulting in the redesigning of the headwear and the dress for the deity. Every attempt is, however, made to adhere to the traditional dress patterns as they appear in the well-known paintings of Radha and Krishna.

Dance and Music: The Puranas describe the proficiency of Krishna in dance and music, Shri Radha in dance, Shri Lalita playing the Veena and Shri Vishakha playing the drums (mridang). The dance and music forms of contemporary Braj have sought to keep alive this rich heritage. Dhrupad, a style of vocal classical music, was given a new form by Swami Haridas, and Braj has become the main centre for the dhrupad style of devotional music.

The folk music of Braj is equally fascinating, with a wide range including group singing of devotional songs in the *Samaj* or the temples. There are folk songs for each season, the most popular being the festive songs of Holi and '*rasia*'.[113]

152. A phoolbangla maker. Phoolbangla is a popular form of temple decoration in summer.

153. Phoolbangla at Bihariji Temple, Vrindavan.

154. Phoolbangla at Radharaman Temple, Vrindavan.

155. Wall painting in Gopi Natl
Ki Haveli, Vrindavan.

156. Wall painting in Raja Suraj M
Ki Chhatri at Kusumsarovai

157. Episodes from the life of Sh
Krishna: a wall painting
Nandgaon Temple.

" भगवान श्री कृष्ण द्वारा माखन चोरीलीला करना "

158. Sunset. Vrindavan — Sanjhi art is open to public only after sunset for the worshippers in the temples.

159

160

159. Sanjhi drawn with colour powder on mud surface at Radharaman Temple, Vrindavan.

160. Samaj Gayan — singing songs in praise of Shri Radha and Sanjhi.

161. Radharaman Temple, Vrindavan. Making snakes with colour powder in circular movement is a most intricate display of the Sanjhi art.

162. Sanjhi: rectangle format with delicate flower motif.

161

162

163

Ras: A contribution of the devotees in the sixteenth century,[114] *Ras leela* is a folk style of dance accompanied by devotional music in praise of Radha and Krishna presented in the form of a dance drama portraying the life and legend of Shri Krishna. This form was initiated by Shri Vallabhacharya and perfected by Shri Narayan Bhatt later.[115] A special feature of the 'ras' is the all male cast, selected largely from children below the age of fifteen years.

Houses of ras organisers (called rasdhari) were formed to select and train boys in dance, acting and music specifically for the ras performance. The tradition is still maintained. The earliest ras is said to have been performed at Kamai and Karhela.[116]

The ras leela when performed has highly religious overtones. The audience stays spellbound throughout the performance. In fact it is a combination of two performances in one. The first part is 'ras' performed as a group dance with Shri Radha and the gopis and Krishna as the only male figure in the group. This style of dance has also been known as 'Halleesaka Kreedana'. This is the dance form identified by the commentators of the 12th century as a dance in which several female forms danced with a hero in the centre. The 'leela' part, which follows ras, covers any one of the episodes concerning the life of Shri

164

165

163. Details of the flower motif.

164. Sanjhi, the temple art.

165. Paper stencil for Sanjhi. Private collection of Harish Chandra Seth of Mathura.

166

167

166. The Sanjhi art requires patience, perseverance and precision.

167. Brass stencil for Sanjhi. Private collection of Harish Chandra Seth of Mathura.

Radha and Krishna. For example, the leela around Krishna's birthday would be centred around the rôle of Kans who imprisoned his sister Devaki and brother-in-law Vasudev. During the festive season of 'Holi' the ras may cover the pranks of Krishna and his cowherds playing Holi with Shri Radha and the gopis.

The religious content in the style and the performance of 'ras' has been nurtured by some of the famous devotees of Shri Krishna. These include names like Vallabhacharya, Shri Hitharivansh, Swami Haridas and many others. The tradition of how the ras would be performed was set by Swami Ghamanddevji. Shri Narayan Bhatt was the one who helped in the growth of the ras form, and thus institutionalising the ras as practised today.

There are several ras mandlies or groups which perform ras almost throughout the year. In Braj, ras is usually staged at the time of the rains commensurate with the festivities of Krishna Janmashtami and in the month of March commensurate with the Holi festival. The performance of ras in the presence of admiring devotees of Krishna reaches its crescendo when thousands of spectators walk past the Yugulsarkar (Radha and Krishna) with affection and veneration.

Chirkula:[117] The village Umri Rampur in Mathura district was the first to develop this dance, performed usually on the full-moon night of the Holi festival. Chirkula is a three to four-tiered wooden frame, with small oil lamps soldered on each frame. The whole contraption weighs about 50 kg. A village belle skilfully balances the lit Chirkula on her head and dances to the accompaniment of folk songs and the rhythm of drums and cymbals, creating a sensational impact on the audience.

Paintings: The theme of Radha and Krishna has provided inspiration for a large variety of art forms. In Braj, these forms are mostly seen as wall paintings, either in the houses of the devout and the rich or in temples. Even today some of the haveli-style temples of 'Pushtimarg' in Braj and neighbouring areas have these wall paintings. These paintings were originally made with natural vegetable colours. The themes cover different aspects of the Krishna legend, the killing of demons like Putna, Bakasur, Kalianag and the frolics of the child Krishna. Most wall paintings in Braj date back to over 100 years. However, with the passage of time many are losing the lustre and vividness of their original colours.

In certain old havelies in Vrindavan one can see some of the paintings, though in a bad state of preservation. The ceiling of the temple of Sheshashai Vishnu has paintings dating back to the late

168

168. Sanjhi `folk art made with cowdung. usually by teenage girls.

169. Sanjhi with flower decoration.

170. Sanjhi Kot. The most detailed configuration is made on the tenth (last) day of Sanjhi festival.

171. Sanjhi Kot.

169

170

171

172. Chirkula. Three to four tiers of wooden frame with oil lamps soldered on each frame. The total weight of the contraption is 40-50 kg.

173. Chirkula dance: a close view.

174. The dancer and the music director.

172

173

177

175. A Krishna Swaroop for ras.

176. Yugul Chhabi. The divine couple is the adored form seen in any ras performance.

177. Maharas: a wall painting at Kokila Van Temple.

178. Hands raised in veneration for Shri Radha: a scene from a ras.

eighteenth century. The most well-preserved wall paintings are those adorning the ceiling of the Chhatri of Raja Surajmal at Kusumsarovar and the temple of Dwarkadheesh at Mathura. The wall paintings on the Chhatri of Raja Surajmal, painted some two hundred and fifty years ago, cover aspects of the Radha-Krishna legend and also depict certain scenes from the royal house of Bharatpur. Most of the wall paintings and the miniature paintings of the different schools (Kangra, Basohli, Mewar, etc.) drew their inspiration from Shrimad Bhagvat, the poetry of Surdas as well as works such as *Geet Govind* of Jai Dev and *Rasik Priya.*

In recent years there has been a revival of interest in wall paintings as evident from the decoration of the walls of the temple at Janmabhumi and the Shriji temple at Barsana. Talented sadhus who have inherited this old art tradition have been engaged in this restoration and redecoration work. The wall paintings of the temple at Kokilavan done by a sadhu have been beautifully executed.

180

179. Dance drama Veni Gunthan: Krishna plaiting Shri Radha's hair.

180. Krishna of Sharad ras, usually performed on the full moon night of autumn.

181. Kans Leela: dance drama enacting the killing of Kans.

182. Shri Radha and Krishna: Ek Pran Do Deh. The popular vision of the Divinity.

181

183. Shri Radha Krishna and the gopis. Each ras performance begins with puja and darshan of Shri Radha and Krishna.

REFERENCES

1 *Kalyan*, Special Issue, 1970-71, "Gargasamhita", Gita Press, Gorakhpur, ch. 3, v 33.
2 Acharya Sharma, Shri Ram, *Skandapuran*, Sanskrit Sansthan, Khawaja Press, Bareilly, Rev. ed. 1984, verse 21.
3 *Kalyan*, 1970-71, "Gargasamhita", op. cit., ch. 3, v 34.
4 Wilson, H.H., *Vishnu Puran*, A system of Hindu mythology and tradition, Punthi Pustak Publication, Calcutta, 3rd ed. 1972, ch. 13, p. 76.
5 *Kalyan*, 1970-71, "Gargasamhita", op. cit., ch. 3, v 35.
6 *Shrimad Bhagavata*, Vol. 2, Gita Press, Gorakhpur, 1951, Canto 10, ch. 11, v 36.
7 *Kalyan*, Special issue, Jan. 1959, "Harivansh Puran", Gita Press, Gorakhpur, v 27.
8 Acharya Sharma, Shri Ram, *Skandapuran*, op. cit., v 20.
9 *Shrimad Bhagavata*, Vol. 2, op. cit., Canto 10, ch. 11, vv 36-37.
10 *Padam Puran* (Patal Khand), Gopal Printing Works, Calcutta-6, 1st ed. 1958, ch. 69, vv 63-71.
11 *Kalyan*, 1970-71, "Gargasamhita", op. cit., ch. 3, vv 24-27.
12 Mishra, Durga Shanker, *Raskhan Ka Amar Kavya*, Navyug Granthagar Mahanagar, Lucknow, 2nd ed. 1965, p. 41.
13 *Kalyan*, 1970-71, "Gargasamhita", op. cit., ch. 6, vv 26-28.
14 *Shrimad Bhagavata*, Vol. 2, op. cit., Canto 10, ch. 11, v 40.
15 Shri Aurobindo and Mother, *Shri Krishna*, Shri Aurobindo Society in arrangement with Shri Aurobindo Ashram Trust, Pondicherry, 2nd ed. 1988, p. 13.
16 *Bhagavat Gita*, Gita Press, Gorakhpur, 1962, 8th ed., ch. 4, v 7.
17 *Chhandogya Upanishad*, Gita Press, Gorakhpur, 1st ed. 1973, ch. 3, v 17.
18 *Shrimad Bhagavata*, Vol. 2, op. cit., Canto 10, ch. 11, v 25.
19 *Kalyan*, 1970-71, "Gargasamhita", op. cit., ch. 14, v 3.
20 Shri Aurobindo and Mother, *Shri Krishna*, op. cit., p. 13.
21 Mittal, P.D., *Braj Ke Dharam Sampradayon Ka Itihas*, Sahitya Sansthan, Mathura, 1st ed. 1968, p. 219.

184. Salutation to Braj Ke Krishna.

22 *Shrimad Bhagavata,* Vol. 2, op. cit., Canto 10, ch. 31, v 1/41.
23 Bajpayee, Krishna Datta, *Braj Ka Itihas, Part I,* Akhil Bhartiya Braj Sahitya Mandal, Mathura, 1st ed. 1955, pp. 124-175.
24 Growse, F.S., *Mathura: A district memoir,* Asian Educational Services, New Delhi-16, Rev. ed. 1979, pp. 155-156.
25 Ibid., 64.
26 Ibid., 148.
27 Ibid., 53.
28 *Balmiki Ramayan,* Uttara Khand, Gita Press, Gorakhpur, 2nd ed. 1963, v 162/1.
29 *Kalyan,* 1970-71, "Gargasamhita", op. cit., ch. 9, vv 43-44.
30 *Shrimad Bhagavata,* Vol. 2, op. cit., Canto 10, ch. 25, v 23.
31 Goswami, Jeev, *Gopal Champu,* ed. Shyam Das, published by Shri Harinam Sankirtan Mandal, Shridham Vrindavan, 1st ed. 1968, ch. 12, v 65.
32 *Kalyan,* 1970-71, "Gargasamhita", op. cit., ch. 10, v 40
33 Growse, F.S., op. cit., p. 303.
34 Ibid., p. 304.
35 Ibid., p. 304.
36 Bajpayee, K.D., Part I, op. cit., p. 162.
37 Growse, F.S., op. cit., p. 307.
38 Goswami, Rupa, *Laghu Bhagavatamrit,* Krishna Das Baba Kusum Sarovarwale, Vrindavan, 1st ed. 1969, ch. 18, v 7.
39 Ibid., ch. 16, vv 21-29.
40 *Kalyan,* 1970-71, "Gargasamhita", op. cit., ch. 16, v 24.
41 Growse, F.S., op. cit., p. 311.
42 Vijay, *Braj Bhumi Mohini,* Shri Ram Sharma, Raseshwar Sadan, Vrindavan, 1st ed. 1985, p. 207.
43 Mittal, P.D., *Braj Ka Sanskritik Itihas,* Rajkamal Prakashan Pvt. Ltd., Delhi for Sahitya Sansthan, Mathura, 1st ed. 1966, p. 121.
44 Ibid., 124.
45 Ibid., 124.
46 Ibid., 117.
47 Vijay, *Braj Bhumi Mohini,* Shri R. Sharma, op. cit., p. 171.
48 Mittal, P.D., *Braj Ka Sanskritik Itihas,* op. cit., p. 118.
49 Mittal, P.D., *Braj Ke Dharam Sampradayon Ka Itihas,* op. cit., p. 219.
50 *Shrimad Bhagavata,* Vol. 2, op. cit., Canto 10, ch. 8, v 34.
51 *Kalyan,* 1970-71, "Gargasamhita", op. cit., ch. 3, v 35.
52 Ibid., ch. 16, vv 21-29.
53 Harivansh, Hit, *Hit Chaurasi,* Venu Prakashan, Vrindavan, 1st ed. 1963, p. 83.
54 *Shrimad Bhagavata,* Vol. 2, op. cit., Canto 10, ch. 39, vv 40-41.
55 Ibid., Canto 10, ch. 16, v 18.
56 Growse, F.S., op. cit., p. 241.
57 Ibid., p. 245.

58 Ibid., p. 253.
59 Ibid., p. 254.
60 Ibid., p. 50.
61 Mittal, P.D., *Braj Ka Sanskritik Itihas*, op. cit., p. 137.
62 Ibid., p. 137.
63 Vijay, *Braj Bhumi Mohini*, Shri R. Sharma, op. cit., p. 397.
64 Dasa, Dhruva Maharaj, *Vrindavan Dham Ki Jaya*, Entourage Publishing International, Francisco, 1st ed. 1989, p. iv.
65 *Shrimad Bhagavata*, Vol. 2, op. cit., Canto 10, ch. 37, v 5.
66 Ibid., Canto 10, ch. 22, v 1.
67 Ibid., Canto 10, ch. 16, v 1.
68 Mittal, P.D., *Braj Ka Sanskritik Itihas*, op. cit., p. 139.
69 Ibid., p. 134.
70 Ibid., p. 133.
71 Ibid., p. 133.
72 *Padam Puran*, op. cit., ch. 69, vv 170-173.
73 Dasa, Dhruva Maharaj, op. cit., p. 48.
74 Kaviraj, Krishna Das, *Chaitanya Charitramrit*, Madhya Leela, Shri Harinam Sankirtan Mandal, Shridham Vrindavan, 2nd ed. 1980, p. 522, ch. 18, v 68.
75 Acharya Sharma, *Skandapuran*, op. cit., vv 37-38.
76 Mittal, P.D., *Braj Ke Dharam Sampradayon Ka Itihas*, op. cit., p. 153.
77 Growse, F.S., op. cit., p. 89.
78 Mittal, P.D., *Braj Ke Dharam Sampradayon Ka Itihas*, op. cit., p. 201.
79 Ibid., p. 217.
80 Kaviraj, K. Das, op. cit., p. 510, ch. 17, v 181.
81 Growse, F.S., op. cit., p. 75.
82 Mittal, P.D., *Braj Ke Dharam Sampradayon Ka Itihas*, op. cit., p. 263.
83 Uttar Pradesh Braj Ank, Sept. 1984, Information and Public Relations Department, UP, Vol. IV, p. 29.
84 Ibid., p. 99.
85 Ibid., p. 268.
86 Ibid., p. 268.
87 Ibid., p. 268.
88 Ibid., p. 269.
89 *Ras Panchadyai*, Sangved Vidyalaya, Mathura, 1st ed. 1970, vv 6-9.
90 Growse, F.S., op. cit., p. 303.
91 Mittal, P.D., *Braj Ka Sanskritik Itihas*, op. cit., p. 270.
92 Ibid., p. 272.
93 Growse, F.S., op. cit., p. 185.
94 Ibid., pp. 91-183.
95 Ibid., p. 93.

96 Ibid., p. 92.
97 Ibid., p. 92.
98 Mittal, P.D., *Braj Ka Sanskritik Itihas*, op. cit., p. 239.
99 Growse, F.S., op. cit., p. 261.
100 Mittal P.D., *Braj Ke Dharam Sampradayon Ka Itihas*, op. cit., p. 314.
101 Kaviraj, K. Das, op. cit., p. 522, ch. 18, vv 30-31.
102 Mittal, P.D., *Braj Ke Dharam Sampradayon Ka Itihas*, op. cit., p. 264.
103 Ibid., p. 153.
104 Ibid., p. 323.
105 Kaviraj, K. Das, op. cit., p. 525, ch. 18, v 175.
106 Chaturvedi, Sitaram, *Vallabhacharya Aur Pushti Marg*, Hindi Sahitya Kuteer, Varanasi, 1st ed. 1966, pp. 30-31.
107 Mittal, P.D., *Braj Ke Dharam Sampradayon Ka Itihas*, op. cit., p. 301.
108 Ibid., p. 250.
109 *Kalyan*, 1959, "Harivansh Puran", op. cit., v 36.
110 Agarwal, Basudeo Sharan, *Sahitya Vachaspati Seth Kanhyalal Poddar Abhinandan Granth*, published by Akhil Bhartiya Braj Sahitya Mandal, Mathura, 1st ed. 1956, p. 332.
111 Ibid., p. 203.
112 Ibid., p. 212.
113 Mittal, P.D., *Braj Ke Dharam Sampradayon Ka Itihas*, op. cit., p. 594.
114 Bajpayee, Krishna Datta, *Braj Ka Itihas, Part II*, Akhil Bhartiya Braj Sahitya Mandal, Mathura, 1st ed. 1958, p. 78.
115 Radha Krishna, *Ras Sarvaswa*, Unpublished, Prathamvidhi.
116 Ibid., Prathamvidhi.
117 Bajpayee, K.D., Part II, op. cit., p. 76.

GLOSSARY

Acharya	Preceptor; head of an academic institution.
Airavat	The mount of Indra, the god of rain and thunder. It means an elephant with many trunks.
Akrur	A devotee of Krishna in his young days at Vrindavan and Mathura.
Arishtasur	A demon slain by young Krishna.
Arti	Ceremony of devotional waving of lamps and other aromatic items in front of the deity.
Aryan	A race of migratory Central Asian tribes who migrated to India.
Avatar	Incarnation.
Bairagi	One who has subdued his worldly desires and passions; an ascetic.
Bajranabh	Great-grandson of Lord Krishna.
Bakasur	A demon disguised as a crane, slain by young Krishna.
Baldev	Lord Krishna's elder brother.
Bhakta	A devotee.
Bhakti	Devotion to God.
Bhagavad Geeta	The battlefield discourses between Lord Krishna and Arjun of the Pandava clan. It is one of the most profound and beautiful philosophical poems in the world.
Brahma	One of the Hindu Trinity composed of Brahma the Creator, Vishnu the Preserver and Shiva the Destroyer.
Charanpahari	Footprints of Krishna on the Govardhan Hill.
Cheerghat	The Yamuna ghat where gopis were having a nude bath. Krishna took all their clothes left on the bank and hung them on a Kadamb tree thus forcing them to beg for the return of the clothes.

Chaitanya Mahaprabhu	An incarnation (as believed by some people) of Lord Krishna who took human birth to teach love of God through the Sankirtan movement.
Dandavati Parikrama	Circumambulation of holy places repeatedly prostrating oneself along the pathway towards the holy spots; pilgrimage.
Dandya	A form of group dance with short sticks in hand to beat varying rhythms of group movement.
Danghati	An opening in the hill ranges of Govardhan.
Deepdan	Offering of lighted lamps.
Dhruv	Son of Uttanpad who ascended as Pole Star as a reward for extreme devotion.
Dwaparyug	The third in the cycle of four Ages, according to Hindu concept. It lasts 864,000 years. The other three Ages are Satyug, Treta, Kaliyug.
Fa-Hien	A Chinese traveller and Buddhist pilgrim who travelled through India in the 5th century A.D. (399-414 A.D.).
Fatehpur Sikri	New Capital city constructed by Mughal Emperor Akbar the Great.
Ganges	India's holiest river which flows from the Central Himalayas to the Bay of Bengal.
Gaudia Sampradaya	The school of Vaishnavism following the teachings of Shri Chaitanya Mahaprabhu.
Gaya	A place of Buddhist pilgrimage in Bihar.
Giriraj	Another name of Govardhan.
Golok	The highest spiritual planet containing Krishna's abodes: Dwarka, Mathura, Vrindavan.
Gops	Krishna's cowherd boy companions; milkmen.
Gopis	Krishna's cowherd women companions; milkmaids.
Goswami	The follower of a particular sect in Braj.
Guru	Spiritual master; revered preceptor.
Govardhan	The hill range which, so the legend says, Krishna lifted on his little finger for seven days to protect the cowherds and cattle from torrential rain.
Hallisak	A special style of dance in Braj. The dancers dance with small sticks in their hands with which they create various designs.
Haridas	A devotee of Krishna and a great musician.
Heracles	A Greek Krishna-like god (in the book of Megasthenes).
Hirnakashyap	A demon king killed by Vishnu, incarnated as half man-half lion.

Holi	Vernal festival known for its conviviality and colours.
Indra	The king of the gods in Heaven. He is known as the god of rain and thunder.
Jagannathpuri	A holy city in Orissa associated with Lord Jagannath.
Jainism	A religion initiated by Shri Mahavir. In India, it ran parallel to Buddhism propagated by Lord Buddha.
Janmashtami	Krishna's birthday.
Jarasandh	Ruler of Magadh and brother-in-law of Kans.
Kadamb	A summer flowering tree, associated with Krishna, gops and gopis.
Kalianag	Serpent dislodged from its lair under the Yamuna by Krishna.
Kans	King of the Bhoj dynasty and maternal uncle of Krishna.
Kirtan	Congregational singing.
Krishna	The incarnation of Vishnu who revealed the Bhagavad Geeta at the battlefield of Mahabharat.
Kurukshetra	The battlefield north-west of Delhi where the battle between Kauravas and Pandavas was fought.
Ladoo Gopal	Lord Krishna as a child with a 'ladoo' (a sweet) in one hand.
Ladliji	Another name of Shri Radha.
Leela	Divine sport.
Leela Sthali	Place of divine sport.
Madan Mohan	An epithet of Lord Krishna, who is the enchanter of even Cupid.
Madhu	A demon slain by Vishnu.
Madhuvan	A forest in Mathura region.
Maharas	The supreme ecstatic dance.
Mirabai	A Rajput princess of Mewar turned devotee of Shri Krishna.
Mukharvind	A head-shaped form of Govardhan.
Mukut	Crown.
Murti	Icon; image; idol.
Nand	Foster-father of Lord Krishna.
Nandgaon	The village to which Nand and his clan migrated from Gokul.
Narada	A devotee of the Lord who travels throughout the universe in his ethereal body glorifying the Lord through devotional music.
Narsingh	Vishnu's man-lion incarnation.

Nimbarka	Religious leader and founder of the Dvaitadvaita school.
Padyavali	A collection of poems.
Pandavas	Yudhishtara, Bhim, Arjun, Nakul and Sahadev — the five sons of King Pandu.
Panini	The celebrated authority on Sanskrit grammar in ancient times.
Parikrama	Circumambulation.
Parmatma	Lord Vishnu as the supersoul supposed to be present within the heart of every living being.
Pitrapaksh	Fortnight during which offerings are made for deceased ancestors.
Prahlad	Son of King Hirnakashyap and a great devotee of Vishnu.
Puja	Devotion; worship of idols.
Putna	A demon-woman slain by infant Krishna.
Radha	Lord Krishna's most intimate consort, who is the personification of His internal spiritual potency.
Radhaashtami	Birthday of Shri Radha.
Rakshasas	Demons.
Ram	An incarnation of Vishnu as the perfect king and man.
Ramanuj	The founder of one of the four Vaishnav Sampradayas.
Ras	The expression in group dance of spiritual love between Krishna and the cowherd damsels of Brajbhumi.
Ras Shiromani	An epithet of Lord Krishna. It means presiding deity of ras.
Raval	Birthplace of Shri Radha.
Ravan	Sri Lanka's powerful demon king who was killed by Lord Ram.
Samadhi	Trance, or absorption in the Lord.
Seva	Devotional service.
Saligram	A stone with sacred markings symbolises Vishnu just as the Shivalinga symbolises Shiva.
Shankaracharya	The incarnation of Lord Shiva (so it is believed) who, ordered by Supreme Lord, propagated the famous Mayavada philosophy, which maintains that there is no distinction between the Lord and his loving entities.
Shiva	One of the Hindu Trinity (Trimurti).
Shringar	Decorating and dressing up the deity.
Stupa	Buddhist relic mound.

Tarnavrat	A demon disguised as whirlwind. He was slain by Krishna.
Tirthas	Places of pilgrimage,
Tulsi	The sacred plant whose leaves were dear to Krishna; also identified as consort of Shri Krishna.
Udhav	An early friend of Shri Krishna. He believed in Gyan instead of Bhakti.
Vaishnavism	One of the sects the followers of which are devotees of Lord Vishnu and his incarnations including Krishna.
Vasudev	Father of Krishna.
Vrinda	Holy basil plant, also, a name for a consort of Krishna.
Vrindavan	A forest township in district Mathura in North India. Radha and Krishna performed most of their leelas there.
Yadavas	Lord Krishna's clan.
Yam	The god of death.
Yashoda	Foster-mother of Lord Krishna.
Yashodanandan	An epithet of Krishna. It means son of Yashoda.

INDEX